SPIRITED LEADERSHIP

SPIRITED LEADERSHIP

Empowering People
to Do What Matters

THOMAS G. BANDY

CHALICE
PRESS
ST. LOUIS, MISSOURI

Scripture quotations marked RSV are from the *Revised Standard Version of the Bible,* copyright 1952 [2nd edition, 1971], by the Division of Christian Education of the National Council of the Churches of Christ in the United States of America. Used by permission. All rights reserved.

Cover art: GettyImages
Cover and interior design: Elizabeth Wright

Visit Chalice Press on the World Wide Web at
www.chalicepress.com

10 9 8 7 6 5 4 3 2   08 09 10 11 12 13

Library of Congress Cataloging-in-Publication Data

Bandy, Thomas G., 1950-
  Spirited leadership : empowering people to do what matters / by Thomas G. Bandy.
      p. cm.
  ISBN 978-0-8272-3468-0
  1. Leadership–Religious aspects–Christianity. 2. Christian leadership. 3. Change–Religious aspects–Christianity. 4. Organizational change. 5. Organization. I. Title.
  BV4597.53.L43B35 2008
  253–dc22

2007037302

Printed in the United States of America

Contents

Welcome

This book shares what I have learned from over ten years consulting with churches about organizational change. Ever since *Christian Chaos* first appeared, the demand for organizational coaching has accelerated. This is true not only among churches, but also among nonprofit, health care, social service, municipal, educational, small business, and even corporate sectors.

As the demand for organizational coaching increased across all sectors of public life, I found myself wondering why such interest was growing in what is, admittedly, a relatively unglamorous topic. I discovered two reasons.

First, all sectors have experienced more than a decade of preoccupation–and perhaps even obsession–with leadership development. No doubt, the role of leadership has changed in the emerging world, and leadership is crucial to the casting of any vision and the accomplishment of any mission. What is new is that we have discovered it is not enough. Leadership by itself has not sustained high-impact mission. The charismatic and dynamic leaders who built great organizations are now retiring, redeploying, or dying. Their imminent departure creates a vacuum that reveals that the organizational models they managed to ignore, circumvent, or merely streamline are still in place and just as ineffective as they were before. No matter how we fret over leadership succession, organizations fundamentally lack confidence that the mantle of authority and the power of permission can simply be inherited, transferred, or bestowed on the next genius in line.

We have moved from an era in which the face of the president or senior pastor was the first image to see on the organizational Web site, to an era in which their faces *never* appear on the Web sites. The successful, colorful, authoritative *leader* has been replaced by the successful, effective, entrepreneurial *team*. Unfortunately, this very lack of visibility has invited all manner of abuses that the traditional bureaucracies and hierarchies could not address.

Therefore, the second reason the demand for organizational coaching has increased is that organizations in all sectors have finally realized that only *radical organizational change* will do. We thought we could escape the necessity of radical organizational change by trusting brilliant leaders to find the shortcuts. Eventually, we realized such shortcuts do not exist. Neither does a way to avoid the pain. The typical organizational structures that emerged from the Enlightenment, and were "perfected" through the nineteenth and early twentieth centuries, are fundamentally and fatally flawed. We have to find a better way to hold leaders accountable for long-lasting, high-impact mission. We must discover a repeatable, predictable, manageable method to get "stuff" done in a timely, responsible, and effective way.

This rebuilding of organizational life is painful, because it does not start with restructuring. It cannot be accomplished simply by redeploying staff, reprioritizing tasks, revising bylaws, or rewriting constitutions. It starts with rebuilding our personal attitudes, reshaping our lifestyles, and realigning our most precious personal and public goals. It requires a different philosophy of doing business.

After over ten years of coaching the servant-empowering organizational model, I have discovered that it all comes down to a moment of *kairos*. This is a moment in time in which you are suddenly thunderstruck by the obvious. What has been staring you in the face suddenly becomes clear. The penny drops. The lights go on. You say "Aha!" From that moment forward, all the complexities become simple; and all the ambiguities are resolved. "Of course!" you say.

Usually this *kairos* moment only comes *after* I have spent endless hours explaining the model, answering questions, and repeating a handful of key principles over and over again in a variety of contexts. Occasionally, the moment of *kairos* has already occurred, and the people gathered in the seminar are simply learning how to work out the details. More often than not, however, the people *think* they've got it, but do not really get it. It's only toward the end that, hopefully, seminar participants suddenly look up with wide eyes and exclaim "Oh!" as if they were just bitten by a bug.

The experience of coaching the servant-empowering organization is like a variation of the old joke about the cowboy introduced to a camel. The "cowboy" is the CEO, senior pastor, school superintendent, or health care administrator who has been riding the old organizational "horses" all his or her life…and has probably grown up on a steady diet of Baby Boomer literature on assertive leadership. The cowboy looks at the camel and says, "My, what an unusual horse!"

"It's a camel," I say.

"It looks like an odd horse," comes the reply.

"It's a camel," I say. "It isn't anything like a horse. It eats differently, lives differently, travels differently, and kicks differently. It's not a horse."

The cowboy walks around the camel with supreme confidence. "I've been riding horses all my life," he says, "and I know horseflesh. If it runs on four legs, carries a rider, is covered with hair, travels in a herd, and attracts flies, it's a horse…or just like a horse…or as good as a horse. It's a horse."

So the cowboy loads the camel with the bridle and saddle of a horse, piles all the tools of his trade into the saddlebags made for a horse, gives the camel a drink from the bucket and a pinch of the spurs, and gallops away as fast as he can to beat the competition. And he succeeds! He crosses the finish line first. He makes his millions and retires. He grows his productivity, or membership, or status in the community, and ranks on the top ten list of large successful firms. What does it matter if the camel dies? Or the saddle slips? Or there is no mount for the next leg of the race?

"Have you got anymore of those funny looking horses?" he asks me.

"It's a camel," I say. "And if you only understood that it *is* a camel, and *not* a horse, you would still be in the race."

In the same way, organizational leaders take my seminar and are introduced to the servant-empowering organization. Out of their addictive habits and preconceptions, it looks like an odd version of the old organizational model. The terminology, like the "humps" on a camel, seem a bit strange and out of place, but they become familiar with it and use it quite intelligibly. Watching them apply the principles of the servant-empowering organization to their particular sector or context is like watching the cowboy saddle a horse. They behave in the old assertive Boomer ways, burden the new organization with revised bylaws and bureaucracies, and charge off to accomplish the brainstorm-of-the-month that is going to beat the competition. They wink knowingly at their colleagues and say, "You know, it's really just a better horse."

Occasionally, however, younger generations in particular, who are more used to walking on their own two legs to get around, will examine the beast more closely. They will notice that this is a beast that will go for days on end without stopping at an oasis for a day off, a longer coffee break, or a pat on the head. It will survive the desert, won't just lay down contentedly when things are going well. It can carry far more tools and equipment, without complaining, than anyone could imagine. It provides stable, steady transportation across all kinds of cultural terrain. And most importantly, it can sustain itself on the water of its own vision, travel in mixed company without getting lost, arrive at the destination it set out to reach, and with only a short rest start all over again.

The camel is designed to travel in a caravan. It is designed to toil uncomplainingly, along winding and dusty roads, bearing heavy burdens, cooperating efficiently with other camels. There is no competition among glossy "stallions" to become the alpha male of an otherwise untamed herd. Camels are never called "proud." The boardroom does not feature portraits of individual camels smiling down from its wall. No one composes poems to eulogize a camel in the corporate mythology. This is because camels are almost never pictured *alone*. They are always in a *caravan*.

This beast may not win the race to be among the "Fortune 500" companies every year. It may not win the philanthropic promotion of former presidents or be pictured as a thoroughbred beside a handsome, smiling, athletic, charismatic, assertive, CEO with a trophy in hand. Yet it will be a steady producer, capture the imagination of serious charitable interests, and receive consistent honorable mentions whenever anything good has happened in the world. The vitality of this organization will not rise or fall depending on what genius leader runs the company this year. Rather, vitality will depend on the organization's own integrity, efficiency, and productivity. Therefore, the organization will always choose a leader who first and foremost will serve the organization.

Once people have had a good look at the beast, eventually someone will interrupt the seminar with an exclamation. "You know, that's not really a horse at all!" they will say. "It's a camel!"

Now, after that blessed event, the teaching can begin.

Tom Bandy

First Things First

The Mission Attitude

The Foundation of Trust

Boundary Thinking

Policy Governance

The Basic Structure

First Things First

Ten years ago, my book *Christian Chaos* was aimed at faith-based organizations. Today, *all organizations are faith-based organizations,* whether or not organizational leaders admit it. Increasing numbers of organizational presidents, CEO's, COO's, and other executive officers *are* admitting it and looking for ways to redefine and network the essential *spirituality* of their organization.

Once, organizational leaders deliberately sought to separate themselves from extraneous "spiritual" interests. Their organization was not in business to protect sacred dogmas, or even to bless the world. It existed to "make money," "manufacture a product," "improve the lot of employees," "accomplish *this* particular task with excellence," "preserve a heritage," and so on. Ironically, even churches separated organizational management from ministries of word, sacrament, and pastoral care. Trustees and board members emulated their secular counterparts. "If only the church were run like a business, we wouldn't be in such a benevolent mess." And so they became a business and made a bigger mess.

The second irony is that while many church leaders are *still* thinking they ought to separate themselves from extraneous "spiritual" interests, many profit and nonprofit organizational leaders are realizing that separation from "spiritual" interests is not only impossible but undesirable. If "productivity" becomes more important than "people," then "program management" will absorb so much energy that "leadership development" will fail. That is precisely what has happened in modernity. That is precisely what emerging organizational leaders refuse to let happen in postmodernity.

"Leadership development" requires "people development." People cannot be separated from the larger matrix of life. That matrix is infused with spiritual interest. No scalpel is sharp enough and no algorithm complex enough to separate culture from faith. Organizations that ignore this fact are doomed to win battles, but lose wars; thrive one year, and go bankrupt the next; capture the imagination of the public for two years, and fade into oblivion. The organizations that thrive in the postmodern world are not obsessed with the "bottom line." They are obsessed with the "inner heart." Success does not depend on program management, no matter how far it quests for quality. It depends on leadership development.

The Spirituality of an Organization

Organizations *are* in the business of protecting sacred boundaries, and they *are* in it to bless the world. They are doing this because it is *good business.* The more they invest in people development, rather than product development, the more they are inextricably bound up in the culture, the environment, and the matrix of life in which people exist and from which leaders emerge. They are not managing a "business," but a tentacle of life that is "connected" to everything else. The *spirituality* of an organization consists of four things: unconditional loyalty, ultimate concern, sacred boundaries, and credible authority.

Unconditional Loyalty

An organization must have something that demands absolute obedience from every member of the organization, from the president to the accountant, or from the pastor to the custodian. Call this "God." This unconditional loyalty must be rewarded by concrete experiences of acceptance in which any and every organizational member feels included in the magnanimity of "God." Call this "covenant." Unconditional loyalty is a fundamental organizational dynamic of obedience and covenant. This very ancient concept is still around because it works. It helps organizations keep going, survive setbacks, reform themselves, and maintain market share.

Most modern organizations operated under *conditional* loyalty, demanded by the skepticism, pragmatism, and individualism of the age. Organizational life was a continuous internal renegotiation, as unions vied with management, employees struggled for benefits, and executives looked for better jobs somewhere else. Organizations became so busy renegotiating the minimum necessities to keep people that they failed to invest in the maximum requirements to grow people, causing generations of postmoderns to opt out entirely.

Every organization does have a dynamic of unconditional loyalty, but for most organizations (including churches) their "God" is not deserving enough and their "covenant" is not affirming enough. It is not easy for organizational leaders to discern what is *really* claiming unconditional loyalty in their organization. They have lived so long in an age of skepticism that they deny the very possibility of the unconditional. Yet it is there. When revealed to objective scrutiny, their "God" is discovered to be weak, ambiguous, and unworthy for anyone to consider surrendering their lives to it.

This "God" may be identified as a person or a principle, but it is so powerful, so obviously beneficial, so all-embracing, and so captivatingly awesome that it demands—and receives—unconditional loyalty. Once recognized, every organizational member is faced with a simple question: "Am I in or am I out?" This is not to say that negotiations will not take place within the organization. It does not assume that everyone will always be uniformly happy, all the time, with their organizational role, remuneration, and relationships. Yet it implies that there is an "inner heart" for the organization's identity and purpose. In the final analysis, continued involvement in the organization is not determined by conditional issues of salary and benefits, but by unconditional loyalties that hinge on the credibility of "God" and the acceptance of "covenant."

Ultimate Concern

The organization must have a cause and a public that form the inspiration and motivation for everything done in the organization. It is a *concern* that drives the innovation and implementation processes of the organization. It is an *ultimate* concern because everything is evaluated, and success is measured, in reference to that cause and that public.

The "cause" inspires the organization in all of its layers and complexities. It shapes the message, the content, and the product. It also shapes the methods in which these things are developed and delivered. The "cause" is a great purpose, a huge issue, an overarching anxiety, and a desperate yearning. The "cause" transforms an organization from an institution into a movement. It is the reason employees come early and stay late. It is the reason church members plan vacations around worship, rather than worship around vacations. They are part of an urgent crusade, in which every minute counts and every sidetrack is blasphemy.

The "public" motivates the organization to be relevant. This is the microculture or segment of the global population that has been defined and targeted to receive the peculiar blessing that the organization is best equipped to impart. The organization does what it does because it really and truly *loves*, and does everything possible to reach, *those particular people.* Organizational members may or not be among "those people," but they have a "heartburst" of compassion for those people, and are often found mingling with "those people" in their free time.

Ultimate concern has become the most concrete way employees or organizational members decide if they are "in or out." Why work for an organization if you don't care enough about its cause to shape your lifestyle around it? Why work for an organization if you don't really love the people the organization is trying to reach? This fundamental convergence of "my life" with "organizational purpose" is how postmodern people separate authenticity from hypocrisy. They have discovered that they simply cannot live as a hypocrite—even a well-paid hypocrite. Moreover, organizational leaders, and organizational teams, do not want to work with hypocrites— even highly-skilled hypocrites. It only takes one hypocrite to cancel out the efforts of dozens of authentic servants. Yet if the entire organization shares the ultimate concern, even the most ambitious strategic plans can be accomplished.

Sacred Boundaries

An organization must have boundaries for organizational behavior that are protected and revered. It is not just that they protect human rights, legal obligations, and financial honesty. Sacred boundaries preserve the integrity of the organization. They ensure that ultimate concern *remains ultimate*. They test the loyalties of organizational members to make sure they are *unconditional* when and where they must be unconditional   and flexible when and where they must be flexible. Sacred boundaries are sacred because they help organizational leaders discern what is crucial and what is not.

As we shall see, sacred boundaries come in various tiers of identity and policy governance. What is of fundamental importance, however, is that these boundaries be recognized as the foundation of trust. Sacred boundaries are the explicit policies and processes that spell out the expectations of "covenant" among organizational members. They provide a reasonable basis for organizational members to trust one another to be imaginative and creative.

Think of sacred boundaries in the ancient context of the temple precinct. Organizational members are free to think and act within the boundaries. It is a reasonable sign of their unconditional loyalty and ultimate concern. However, if they go beyond the boundaries, the reason to trust is broken. The physical features of the temple precinct have been replaced by policies or processes that can be taken anywhere, in any context.

What makes a boundary "sacred" is that it is tested against, and subject to, the unconditional loyalty and ultimate concern of the organization. When an organization denies the existence of an unconditional loyalty, or when an organization is unclear about its ultimate concern, then policies and processes become mere by-laws and legalisms. Not only is creativity stifled, but trust itself breaks down. The interpretation of boundaries becomes subject to the whim of committees, the intimidation of controllers, or the impositions of the state. Truly "sacred" boundaries transparently reveal what is unconditional and ultimate in organizational life.

Credible Authority

An obvious and direct connection exists among unconditional loyalty, ultimate concern, sacred boundaries, and credible authorities. In the emerging spirituality of all postmodern organizations, leadership has a "priestly" quality. That is to say, organizational leaders obtain their authority and maintain their influence through their intentional alignment with these things. Their authority does not really lie in their office and position, salary and seniority, or even skills and expertise. It lies in their clearly perceived alignment with what is unconditional, ultimate, and sacred in the organization.

To this extent, leadership indeed has something "charismatic" about it. It is charismatic in the original meaning of that word, namely, infused with the "spirit" of the organization. The authority of the leader does not emanate from his or her personality, but from a symbolic identity with the spiritual center of the organization. The leader *is* the organization. If you want to know the unconditional loyalty, ultimate concern, and sacred boundaries of the organization, all you have to do is follow the leader in "real time" for forty-eight hours. You will see it all in her or his behavior.

Credible authority is revealed through policy governance. It is not revealed through tactical management. Authority is best exercised in the servant-empowering organization through maintaining boundaries beyond which people cannot go, rather than by telling people what to do. The former encourages creativity. It demonstrates trust and encourages leadership development. The latter discourages creativity. It demonstrates condescension and encourages program management. The former is respected, and the latter is resented.

This "priestly" character to organizational leadership contributes to the *spirituality* of organizational life. The key to organizational growth, therefore, is not hiring the right people, but mentoring the right people. More time must be spent inculcating the *spirituality* into the next or the new organizational leader. The unconditional loyalty must be encouraged; the ultimate concern must be embedded; the sacred boundaries must be learned. Once the longevity of organizations could be measured in years and decades. Then the mentoring of organizational leaders could be undertaken slowly. Today, the longevity of organizations is measured in weeks and months, and the mentoring of credible authority must be undertaken with urgency.

Conclusion

The *spirituality* of the organization is the first and most foundational aspect of the servant-empowering organization. It is the most frequently ignored (especially by established churches), and it is the most common cause of organizational decline and collapse. Yet when properly addressed, the *spirituality* of the organization can of itself overcome the most severe handicaps of financial resource and public persecution. Victory does not go to the strong, but to the faithful.

Postmodern eyes quickly see that most organizations do not make first things first. First things are a distant second. Tragically, this is nowhere more true than among institutional churches and other supposedly religious organizations. Loyalty is conditional to membership rewards; ultimate concern is narrowed to personal needs; sacred boundaries are blurred by unjustifiable bureaucracy; and credible authority is undermined by unaligned behavior. The restoration of organizational vitality requires more than restructuring programs and redeploying staff. It requires an entire change of attitude. Great leaders do more than increase profits and stabilize benefits. They reshape the heart of the organization.

The Mission Attitude

The servant-empowering organization only works if the leaders and members of the organization are clearly united in a mission. The organization does not exist for itself, or for the financial success or well being of the organizational managers and employees, but for the improved living and positive progress of somebody beyond the organization. That's a mission attitude.

Membership Privilege as the Opposite to Mission Attitude

The best way to understand a mission attitude, and to understand why most organizations in all sectors of public life do not really have one, is to define the opposite. The opposite of a mission attitude is a membership privilege. Most church organizations, for example, are organized to protect membership privilege rather than accomplish any particular mission. The members care for one another, prioritize wedding fee structures that benefit themselves, design worship and music to honor their own aesthetic tastes, and protect the particular heritage that they cherish most. If there is any time or money left over, they will give it away to bless other people. First, however, they pay the heating bills and pastoral salaries, take care of their own, and maintain their organizational needs. The organizational constitution and bylaws, and the boards and committees that govern church affairs, are designed to protect membership privileges first and do mission later. Indeed, the best way to do mission is to invite, persuade, convert, or cajole strangers to *become members,* because then they will move to the head of the line and get their needs addressed first.

The selfishness of established churches in North America is becoming an old joke among nonprofit and for-profit leaders, but before you deride the speck in your brother's eye (so to speak), organizational leaders from all other sectors had better examine the log in their own eyes. The truth is that most non-church organizations do not have a mission attitude either.

The translation of "membership privilege" into the language of business and nonprofit organizational life is "market share." "Market share" functions in the same way as "membership privilege" because it is just as self-serving. First, the organization protects its investors and its place amid the competition, and then it takes risks to expand its reach. If there is any downturn in the fortunes of the organization, it will cut productivity, lay off underlings and other nonessential personnel, but heaven forbid the senior executives should take a pay cut! The pension plan will be protected, the office will be united, marketing will get a raise, and the profit margin will be "interpreted"...but Research and Development will be slashed. Work to rule and make sure you get what you deserve.

Most leaders and members of an organization associate a "mission attitude" with "passion," but it is crucial to focus what that "passion" is really for. A mission attitude is not passionate for a public policy, a program, a product, or a legacy. It is not a passion for the environment; or for worship, education, preaching, and pastoral care; or for excellent performing arts, or quality picture frames, or meaningful weddings; or for the essence of being "Lutheran," or manufactured goods that are "made in America." The only attitude that counts as a "mission attitude" is a passion *for people.* Authentic mission connects with real people in their brief journey from birth to death. Mission cares about people more than public policy, and more than excellent programming, and more than heritage.

Mission Attitude as a Passion for People

This passion for people, however, must be refined and focused. A mission attitude is not a passion for people *in general,* but for a specific section of the public *in particular.* This is why the mere investigation of demographics is useless in shaping the servant-empowering organization. A mission attitude is not a passion for a generational group, but for *that particular sub-group of children,* or *youth,* or *middle-age single women,* or *seniors experiencing bereavement in the last eighteen months,* and so on. Consider the major demographic categories of the census. Nobody feels any passion for homeowners in general, or for single people in general, or for youth in general, or for income brackets in general, or for people who have relocated from outside the state in the last five years *in general.* Passion has to do with a particular group of people that is definable, describable, and visible *over there.* It is a passion for *that* group of people, rather than *this* group of people. And the more closely you can describe that group of people, the more passionate you become about them.

Phrased more accurately, a mission attitude has a passion for a "lifestyle segment." There are between 50–60 lifestyle segments frequently identified in North America, and any given zip code will have three or four that seem to be dominant. One might well have a passion for the "desperately poor," or for "young and coming" singles, or for "cross-cultural urban families," for example; but even that is too abstract to shape a mission attitude. The truth is that this passion for a *particular* public must be transformed into a passion for a *peculiarly special* public. They are special *to the organizational leaders and members.* They are so "peculiar" that the organization has invested enormous, enthusiastic research into understanding this particular public that they especially cherish.

Mission with a Heartburst

A public is "particular" because they share a common lifestyle or a common need. A public becomes "peculiar" to a servant-empowering organization because *they are in love with that microculture.* They really, really want to find a way, and do whatever it takes, and take significant risks, to better the lives of those people that they care about so much. I call this passion a "heartburst." The servant-empowering organization has a "heartburst" for a peculiar people. Their collective heart breaks for them. They *yearn* to help them. Their leaders are left sleepless at night trying to imagine new ways to reach them. Their members spend personal and corporate time praying constantly for them. That peculiar public is more important to them than their own families and personal privileges, and they are willing to risk both for the sake of their "heartburst."

My most common observation as a consultant for organizational change is that a church, nonprofit, or for-profit organization generally *does not really have a "heartburst,"* or to say it another way, their collective "heart" only "bursts" for themselves. They may talk a good line about being friendly to newcomers, caring about the environment, and being concerned for the poor; but the truth is that worship powerfully motivates them to little more than to go home to lunch and pre-authorize 1 percent of their *net* income to charity. They will shake their heads sadly about starvation in Africa, but what really gets them incensed enough to shout at meetings and fistfight in the hallways will be some perceived breach of their membership privileges. Nobody ever left a traditional church in a huff because the organization failed to send their own congregational missionaries for Tsunami relief to Asia, but they will leave in a huff if the pastor fails to visit them in the hospital.

The same observation can be made for many nonprofit organizations of all charitable varieties. They often start out with a "heartburst" for victims of a disease, lost generations, addicted people, species on the brink of extinction, and so on. Before long their real passion is to advocate public policy, lobby congress, raise money, protect ownership of programs from imitators, keep volunteers happy, or protect the salaries and benefits of the employees. The consultant begins to hear stories about bureaucracy, inflexibility, indifference, cultural insensitivity, lack of availability, and so on, from the very constituency the charity was created to reach. Phone the receptionist, talk to a secretary, converse with the custodian, interact with a nurse, argue with a harried case worker, and just try to schedule an appointment with the CEO and the *particular* public realizes they are no longer *peculiar* to the organization. No sign of a heart bursting appears anymore–only the clickety-clack of a well-oiled machine.

The same observation can also be made for many for-profit organizations. It may seem odd that I even mention "for-profits" in this discussion. The major employers in my small city are an automobile parts manufacturer with several factory locations and a microbrewery that has grown to national distribution. How does a collective "organizational heart" burst over manufacturing brake pads or brewing amber ale? Yet that is exactly what *must* happen if the company wants to transform itself from a "horse" into a "camel"…from a traditional hierarchical organization into a servant-empowering organization, and from a profit-making task machine into life-sustaining contributor to the well-being of the world.

The Power of Mission Attitude

Now, it might be said that this auto parts manufacturer and brewery do not really *want* to be servant-empowering organizations. That's fine. Find a consultant who can help you streamline a traditional hierarchy, resolve conflicts with various unions, and improve efficiency. "Total quality management" is just what you need. But is it? More and more corporate presidents and CEOs are discovering that they are also real human beings. They have real worries and concerns about where the world is going. They discover a real connection between the long-term success of their business and improving the well-being of the world. If nothing else, both the Asian and European markets have demonstrated over and again that employers and employees are more productive and more successful when they are united in a passion for a peculiar public, and not just putting in time to get paid.

Is it possible that a "mission attitude" might actually improve a business? What would happen if the corporate executives, middle managers, and assembly line workers experienced a collective "heartburst" for orphaned children and crippled adults who experienced traffic accidents caused by faulty brakes? What would happen if the entire brewery organization experienced a collective "heartburst" for the physical fitness, emotional stability, and quality of life of the fifty percent of the population that is single at any given time? Would that motivate them to do work better and faster? If organizational leaders encouraged such attitudes, it would alter their marketing strategies. Their companies might better survive the future retirements of senior executives, deal more positively with the complaints of employees, hire more highly motivated managers, and confidently expect to be a presence in the marketplace fifty years from now. Many corporations are indeed shifting to the team-based principles of the servant-empowering organization, but the real key to the success of the transition is *every team must share a collective "heartburst"* for a peculiar public. If not, they will lose their way and fall back into hierarchy.

Mission Attitude as Impact on a Peculiar Public

A mission attitude, however, is more than a passion for a peculiar public. It is a passion to accomplish something with that peculiar public, or, an intention to have a specific impact on that peculiar public. Something positive and measurable is going to happen amid that public if the organization is doing its job. Many organizations have a passion for a peculiar public, immerse themselves in that public, and enjoy dialogue with that public; but when asked what they hope will result from that interaction, they become quite vague. Churches, for example, find ways to include diverse races, languages, and cultures in their worship services and programs. They boast of good relationships with other community leaders. They mingle easily with various neighborhoods and lifestyles. Nevertheless, all that "mingling" in the neighborhood is essentially purposeless. They have no clear idea what they hope to accomplish.

TRANSFORMATION

A mission attitude is an overall purposefulness. That purpose is two-fold. First, the mission attitude desires to *transform* that peculiar public. A mission attitude is never, ever neutral toward a peculiar public for whom its collective heart bursts. A mission attitude sets out to change people. This will not be a superficial change. It is not just the introduction of various programs, or the temporary solution to various needs. It is a change to the habits, attitudes, expectations, and the very lives of the peculiar people that you cherish. Organizational leaders will need to shape exactly how that transformation will take place and what it will look like in response to the context of the peculiar public. We will talk about that later in this book. Is there a danger that this "mission attitude" could become too intrusive and even offensive to the peculiar public that they love so much? Of course! This is always a risk the organization is willing to make. It is literally the risk inherent in all loving relationships. The organization can guard against such intrusiveness through constant dialogue with the public and by rigorous accountability within the organization.

Many churches and all kinds of North American organizations harbor a twentieth-century assumption that respect for a segment of the public requires an absolute acceptance of who they are. This has been encouraged by contemporary critiques of imposed "Westernization" in the Third World; or by stories of manipulative "conversion" tactics from abused individuals. These breaches of accountability have led churches and other organizations to go to the opposite extreme of distancing themselves from the lives of real people. They focus on treating the symptoms of pain with superficial social service programs, without bringing healing and transformation to the deeper causes of problems. A few comparisons will demonstrate this attitude and assumption. It is as if...

- parents were to say, "I do not wish to intrude upon the integrity of my children, so I will simply place spiritual literature and condoms on the coffee table, and let them decide for themselves what god to believe in and whether they should practice safe sex with their current friend."
- children were to say, "I do not wish to intrude upon the integrity of my parents, so I will limit myself to occasional phone calls, and let them decide for themselves whether Dad shows the initial symptoms of Alzheimer's and whether Mom should take control of the bank accounts."
- friends were to say, "I do not wish to intrude upon the freedom of my friends, so I'll just drive them home when they get drunk and leave it to them to decide whether or not they are an alcoholic and what they should do about it."
- theists were to say, "I do not wish to offend anybody in my neighborhood, so I'll just keep my beliefs to myself, and let others decide for themselves whether they are wasting their lives and should commit suicide in despair, or whether they are harming others and should persist in their bigotry."

The point is that a "heartburst" demands a deeper, riskier, deliberate, and purposeful interaction with the peculiar public that you cherish. It is all too easy to respect without love. Indeed, in the interests of respect, organizations deliberately refrain from experiencing real love. If you really love someone, you will really get *involved* with someone; and you will become involved for the specific purpose of transforming their lives for the better.

Empowerment

An authentic mission attitude avoids manipulation and abuse because the passion for a peculiar public is not aimed solely at their *transformation*. It is also aimed at their *empowerment*. In other words, a mission attitude equips that cherished public to take responsibility for its own well-being. The mission attitude builds their self-esteem, deepens their confidence, equips them with skills, helps them work together…*and then lets go!* The healing, equipping, and team-building are all very important, and how that happens will again vary as organizational teams customize tactics that are supremely sensitive to any given context. It will be up to board and management to help organizational teams define their strategic plans, and we will talk about this later. The most difficult part of a mission attitude is the daring to "let go of control." This "letting go" allows the peculiar public, for whom your heart bursts, to learn from their own mistakes, experiment with their own ideas, and own their own risks. Several comparisons help us see what this letting go looks like. It is as if…

- caring parents were to say, "We have shared from our hearts, taught you everything we know, helped you clarify what is good, beautiful, and true, and now please leave our house, live on your own, take your own lumps, and find your own way. We love you."
- caring children were to say, "We have helped you face the trials of aging, helped you find as much security as possible, connected you with the best health plans, and reminded you of your faith and hope, and now please have the courage to accept what cannot be changed, live optimistically, and call us only when you really need us. We love you."
- friends were to say, "We have counseled you with our best advice, networked you with experts in whatever specialization you need, told you the truth as we best can see it, and now please stop using me or depending on me, take responsibility for yourself, and get a life. We love you."
- Christians were to say, "We shared our experience of Christ that gives us joy, did all we could to better your world, answered what questions we could answer, and questioned what needed to be challenged, and now please ask and answer your own questions, stake your life on your own convictions, and dare to live in ambiguity that will never go away this side of heaven. We love you."

The point is that a "heartburst" requires letting go of control and allowing the peculiar public that you most cherish the freedom and power to make decisions, initiate actions, and form partnerships that might even seem risky, doubtful, or precarious, because you trust people to do what is in their best interests and to learn from their inevitable mistakes.

Servant-empowering organizations do not merely accept who people are. They have a vision of what a people can become. They love that peculiar public enough to risk helping them become something greater than they already are. They love them enough to risk letting them create a future for themselves that may be different from the future the organization has built for itself. They love them enough to meddle in their affairs.

One of the profound observations from the small business sector is the insight: "Our clients are our best employees." This means that the small business has not only served the client, *and* helped the client serve themselves, *but also* has helped the client multiply the process to help other colleagues. The resources, principles, and skills the client has gained working with the small business not only help them do their own work better, but are passed on to help their own clients, partners, and networks work better as well. The breakthrough insight is that such radical sharing of expertise does not work the original small business right out of a job. Those other colleagues, partners, and networks now turn to the original small business to refine their own resources and skills. They actually *select* that small business from among the competition precisely because of the credibility created among the original set of clients. The small business then evolves to another sphere of influence. They not only create basic resources and teach basic skills, but now become a source for creating more advanced resources and coaching more advanced skills. Suddenly the goal of the small business is not just to "make a buck," but to "coach a community." Their clients are not consumers anymore, but business associates in their own right.

Apply this principle to churches. The traditional church organization that protects membership privileges is designed to draw people into the institution…and make them dependent on the institution. This is why clergy assert a certified professionalism, or an exclusive "sacramentalism," or a denominational authority that cannot be fully shared with the laity. No matter how skilled laity become, they remain dependent on the clergy to preach, lead worship, visit, counsel, represent the church in official settings, resolve disputes, and so on. Leaving the church is a bad thing. Sporadic attendance is a bad thing. Taking initiative without the tactical approval of a board is a bad thing. In every way possible, the institutional church tries to hold onto its people, keep the flock together, and protect their spiritual "market share."

The servant-empowering church, however, has learned the insight of the small business sector. They understand that their members are their best staff persons, and that their adherents are their best missionaries. Empowerment means not only the healing and transformation of people, but also the equipping of people to preach their own sermons, pray their own prayers, solve their own problems, and lead a spiritual life without dependency on the institution. More than this, empowerment also means that the church helps these people give away that "expertise" to neighbors, work associates, and total strangers they meet on the way. No, this does not mean the church works itself out of a job. It is quite the reverse. The church grows. New people come to the church based on the credibility they have observed in the members and adherents. The church not only creates basic resources and teaches basic skills, but now becomes a source for advanced missionary training. Their "clients" are not consumers anymore, but "missionaries." Their goal is not to "survive with integrity," but to "grow in mission."

Mission Attitude as Call

All this reveals a final, crucial piece to the mission attitude. It is a call. As the church learned from the small business sector, now the small business sector learns from the church. The corporate world is rediscovering the nature of vocation or call.

The call is more than a passion. It is a compulsion. It is something you do, even when you wake up in the morning and don't want to do it. You keep doing it in sickness and in health, for better or worse, until death do you part. The "work" and the "life" are not separate spheres anymore. You know you are experiencing a real call when you realize that if you stop working you will stop living—and if you keep living you will inevitably keep working. The call is a noble purpose, beyond your control, that is a primary source of self-esteem and joy. It is the surrender of self, not to profit or prestige, but to the task itself.

We are used to asking ourselves, "What do I want to do with my life?" That is about discerning passion. Yet there is another question to be answered: "What does life want to do with me?" That is about experiencing call. In a Christian context, church leaders ask, "What shall I do with God?" That is about discerning passion. It's about discovering your gifts and talents, training yourself for a task or a role, and finding the career choice that will give you greatest satisfaction. They rarely ask (and answer) the deeper question: "What does God want to do with me?" That is about discerning call. It's about *receiving* gifts that you may not even want, training yourself for tasks that you do not feel inclined to do, and making a career decision knowing that it is contrary to your nature. That is a call.

Conclusion

We have talked about a mission attitude as a passion to transform and empower a peculiar public. What if you do not *like* that public? What if, like Jonah, the last people on earth you feel predisposed to assist are the residents of Nineveh? What if, by helping Nineveh, you risk losing your marriage, your financial stability, your current set of friends, and more lucrative contracts in Rome? That's a call, and the peculiarly painful thing about vocations is that they cannot be resisted. They swallow you whole, just as Jonah, in attempting to escape, was swallowed by the whale. The call carries you away.

Servant-empowering organizations must have a mission attitude. The mission attitude may be defined as *the passion and call to transform and empower a peculiar public.* How an organization arrives at a consensus around that mission attitude, and rigorously aligns its life to pursue that mission attitude, is the next subject.

The Foundation of Trust

The servant-empowering organization is a "high trust" organization, rather than a "constant oversight" organization. Both organizations have accountability, but they go about it quite differently. Traditional "high oversight" organizations require detailed mandates prescribing everything that must or can be done. These organizations provide multiple tiers of supervision to make sure everything gets done in the proper timeline and process mandated by the hierarchy. As we shall see, servant-empowering organizations accomplish work through the equipping and sending of entrepreneurial teams. It encourages creativity, innovation, and adaptability. It is not only comfortable with change, but welcomes and encourages change. The traditional organization values continuity; but in the servant-empowering organization, *if you blink, everything is different.*

Trust within Corporate Culture

Therefore, the servant-empowering organization only works if every participant in the organization has good reason to trust each other. This is not "blind" trust. The organization does not ask people to trust its leaders and teams simply because they hold an office, have an advanced degree, have been certified by a church denomination, or have acquired special expertise. This is not "suspicious trust." The organization does not ask people to trust its leaders and teams *to a point,* and then demand constant information sharing and administrative liaisons to "check up" on each other. Trust in the servant-empowering organization is "reasonable trust." It is the confidence that all members of the organization (leaders and teams), no matter how innovative and creative they might be, will always behave in certain predictably positive ways.

The term often applied to behavioral expectations within an organization is "corporate culture." Every organization has a peculiar milieu, feel, atmosphere, or habit that is distinctive even from their closest competitors. *This* church feels and behaves differently from *that* church, even though the two churches are just blocks apart and are part of the same denomination. *This* hospital feels and behaves differently from *that* hospital, even though the two institutions are in the same city and perform similar medical procedures. This culture is often unrecognized within the organization, although it is very apparent to outsiders looking in. Organizations often unconsciously hire staff, or welcome newcomers, from within the hidden expectations of this culture, and the culture is perpetuated without any objective analysis. In any sector, the ultimate success or failure of any organization has less to do with their effectiveness in various programs, and more to do with the quality of the organizational culture itself. Shaping that culture has now become more important to corporate, nonprofit, health care, and other sectors than strategic planning.

Ironically, among the organizations across all sectors, the church has remained the most indifferent and insensitive to the issue of congregational "culture." They have relied on generic denominational ethos as a poor substitute. Yet this indifference is also true in large corporations and nationally franchised nonprofits. Companies have relied on national slogans and behavior policies, without giving serious attention to the nuances of culture from one factory, distribution center, franchise, or health unit to the next. It is a crucial error, because organizational culture cannot really be imposed from above. It must be "home grown" from below. It is not dictated by the head office. It is nurtured in dialogue between the senior leaders and the lowly workplace.

Key Issues in Corporate Culture

I first discussed organizational culture at length in my book *Moving Off the Map*,[1] in which I presented an extended process to build clarity and consensus around core values, beliefs, vision, and mission. Two key issues have emerged in the nearly ten years of subsequent organizational coaching that need greater elaboration before we can understand how organizations lay a foundation of trust.

First, many organizations have never seriously studied their own corporate culture. This is especially true of organizations of Western European heritage, and even more especially true of local church congregations of Western European heritage. The obsession with tasks, profits, success, privilege, seniority, pensions, and personal advancement has made these organizations ineffective and noncompetitive, but instead of facing these negative corporate addictions that are undermining organizational life and vitality, these organizations respond simply with quest for quality, more information, and more intrusive supervision. They live in a fog about their real identity, their hidden habits, and their chronic problems. As a result, they become increasingly bogged down by internal conflicts, sudden reversals of tactics, and internal budget competition. Occasionally a new CEO or senior pastor might model a different behavioral norm to bring

---

[1]Thomas G. Bandy, *Moving Off the Map: A Field Guide to Changing Congregations* (Nashville: Abingdon Press, 1998).

more unity and productivity to the organization, but it remains essentially anomalous to the culture. As soon as that leader is gone, the organization reverts to old habits.

Second, in the absence of a culture of trust, there will always be a culture of nontrust. Organizations begin to be shaped around power rather than purpose. Intimidating, manipulative, and sometimes brilliant controllers learn how to work the system for personal or factional self-interest. Organizational members live in an atmosphere of automatic suspicion or skepticism about the motivations and goals of other organizational members. The culture of "nontrust" is often hidden below the surface of seeming success. The propaganda of the company, or the preaching of a church, might extol the unity of the organization and the friendliness of the congregation, but hidden beneath that surface is the reality of backbiting, cynicism, and uncertainty. The leaders may be oblivious, and even believe their own propaganda and preaching. The truth is revealed in the following:

- Low percentages of newcomers, adherents, and new volunteers in the life of a church or high turnover of employees, staff, or volunteers in regular participation in the organization
- Remarkably few stories of any serious and significant innovation or change in the life of the organization
- Little energy invested in researching the needs of the market or listening to the trends of the mission field
- Lack of clarity about grievance processes, combined with high diplomatic energy given to resolving conflicts and disagreements, or providing pastoral care
- Predictable, presentational, passive, and boring worship or tedious, micro-managed, crisis-driven annual meetings and organizational gatherings

All these are signs that, despite what leaders and members think and project, the reality is that they live in a cultural milieu of "nontrust." They do not have a good reason to trust one another, and therefore do not have a plan to empower newcomers quickly and efficiently into positions of real influence and leadership. The median age of the organizational members goes up; the average tenure of membership required to achieve responsible leadership goes up; and the time consumed making even the smallest tactical decision goes up. They don't trust one another.

Elements in the Foundation of Trust

The foundation of trust consists of four things. I first described these in *Moving Off the Map,* and experience has changed the definitions very little. The foundation of trust is a clear consensus across the organization about the following:

- Core Values are the positive, predictable behavior patterns that organizational participants can be expected to model, both spontaneously and daringly, in their daily living.
- Bedrock Beliefs are the principles and convictions to which organizational participants can be expected to turn, immediately and spontaneously, in times of trouble, confusion, or stress.
- Motivating Vision is the "song in the heart" that elicits incredible joy in the lives of organizational participants, shapes the rhythm of their work, and demands to be shared with strangers.
- Strategic Mission is the single, measurable, audacious goal that deserves all the sacrifice and support of organizational members, captures the imagination of the public, and can be printed on the side of a bus.

Together, these four things define the corporate culture of any organization and ultimately determine if that organization will live or die in the long term.

Some things have changed in the last ten years of organizational coaching, however. I see more sharply than ever before how organizations *resist* clarity and consensus in each of these four areas, and I see more urgency than ever before to ruthlessly apply this clear consensus to the behavior of the organization. I am continually astonished at how passionate traditional organizational leaders are about living in a fog. It corresponds to their preoccupation with membership privileges rather than mission urgency. Creating a foundation of trust implies a readiness to let go of control and allow those trusted employees or volunteers real freedom to do things differently than leaders might ordinarily expect. Traditional leaders want to be trusted above all else, but seem to find it quite acceptable not to trust those around them. That must change.

Much of the persistent "fog" surrounding organizational life is unconscious and subtle. Like fog, it pervades all the nooks and crannies of organizational life, from the boardroom to the mail room. Like fog, it reduces and obscures hearing, so that organizational leaders and members simply cannot recognize the obvious. Definitions must be repeated over and over again, as organizational ears strain to comprehend the plain meaning of a sentence.

Core Values

A core value is a positive, predictable behavior pattern that organizational participants can be expected to model, both spontaneously and daringly, in their daily living. The most common resistance to this simple statement is to assume we are speaking about *aspirations*. People think a core value is an ideal that is revealed more in the failure to live up to it, than in the repeated modeling of it. Organizations believe in "peace," but organizational members do not regularly, constantly, and predictably behave "peaceably" with one another, clients, and network partners. They claim to value "love," but do not have any concrete understanding of what "loving behavior" might look like on a daily basis.

Core values are revealed in two ways:

- First, they are revealed in daring, life-risking, acts. For example, a senior corporate executive resigns his highly paid position in the tobacco industry, and takes a lesser job in another company, simply because he has a core value for "health." A nonprofit CEO engages in an act of civil disobedience and willingly goes to jail, simply because she has a core value for "racial equality." A navy chaplain willingly surrenders his life jacket to a crew member and goes down with the ship, specifically because he has a core value for "self-sacrifice." However, daring and life-risking acts are generally avoided when possible, occur rarely, and often surprise even the person who performs the daring deed.
- The second, more reliable way in which core values are revealed is through spontaneous behavior. It is not our intentional deeds or judicious words that reveal our core values, but out spontaneous deeds and our unrehearsed words. Never rely on the strategic planning of an organization to reveal its core values! A pastor may preach about the value of children, but it is only when he, seeking to give a beleaguered mother a respite, spontaneously reaches for a crying baby that might vomit all over his Geneva gown that we see he really does value children. A hospital administrator might espouse the company mission statement about justice for the elderly, but it is only when we watch her walk through the nurses' station cluttered with wheelchairs and interact with each of the patients that we can tell if she really means it. The real organizational core values are revealed in a thousand unplanned ways through the daily behavior of the boardroom and the mail room...the pastor and the custodians...the CEO and the secretaries. And it is revealed when they are "on the job" and "on vacation."

Core values are *positive, predictable behavior patterns that shape the total lives of leaders and members in the organization.* They are not ideals, wishful thinking, or aspirations. It may be that we fail to live up to expectations; but these are expectations that we urgently, desperately, and passionately *desire* to do. If we fail in the attempt, we will feel enormous guilt and seek whatever help we can in order not to fail again. You see these values revealed at home and at play, as well as at work.

The language of "corporate addiction" most readily applies here. Organizations are possessed by self-destructive behavior patterns that they chronically deny. These habits undermine their best intentions and block their highest ideals. Part of the discernment of positive core values is the confrontation of negative core values. The organization is like a recovering alcoholic. The "first step" to change corporate culture is to finally acknowledge the addiction. Then, through constant accountability and mutual support, the organization painstakingly and gradually modifies its predictable behavior pattern. Along the way, some "addicts" who refuse to "come clean" will have to leave the organization; and other "recovering addicts" and healthy people will become attracted to the new, positive experience of the reborn organization.

Bedrock Beliefs

A bedrock belief is a principle or conviction to which organizational participants can be expected to turn, immediately and spontaneously, in times of trouble, confusion, or stress. It is a faith-stance toward life. The most common resistance to this simple statement is to assume we are speaking about *doctrines.* People think a bedrock belief is an abstraction, a perspective, or a point of view that differentiates one organization from another. They live in the illusion that Christians running for their lives as the World Trade Center towers collapsed were automatically reflecting on the doctrine of the Trinity; or that a hopeful mother experiencing problems in labor will focus her mind on proofs for the existence of God. Consider, for example, the following typical list of bedrock beliefs brainstormed by a traditional congregation:

- There is one God eternally in three Persons.
- Faith without works is dead.
- Salvation by grace alone.
- The Bible is uniquely inspired and without error.
- Love one another.
- Prayer is powerful.
- God is love.

None of these abstractions is bedrock. When a businessman recounts his escape from the collapsing Trade Center towers in 2001, he does not recall running down 5th Avenue thinking about the inerrancy of scripture or the doctrine of creation. He finds himself repeating over and over again the words of Isaiah: "Fear not, for I am with you; be not dismayed, for I am your God; I will strengthen you, I will help you, I wiill uphold you with my victorious right hand" (41:10, RSV).

A bedrock belief is a conviction about the significance of life and death, God, purpose, meaning, and what is really important. It is what people turn to for strength when they are in trouble. It is what keeps them sane, gives them hope, and protects them from despair and suicide. The organization is confident that whatever befalls organizational members individually or as a group, and whatever the diversity of individual perspectives and faiths, they will all turn to *this* and *this* to find strength.

- Rescuing children from poverty is worth the risk of one's stability and life.

- Compassion is the attitude of a company rallying around grieving employees.
- Justice is the relentless passion of the universe and this organization.
- A Higher Power can guide you to break addiction and rediscover joy.

A servant-empowering organization has as much corporate clarity about this as it does about core values. Organizational participants must have hope for tomorrow.

It should be obvious how this applies to a church. With a little more thought, it becomes obvious why this should apply to nonprofit organizations in general. The breakthrough insight is the discovery that clarity and consensus about bedrock beliefs is just as important for small business and corporate life. Times of confusion and stress beset businesses on a regular basis in the speed, blur, and flux of postmodern life. The ability to cope with the unexpected now matches the ability to do quality work as essential expectations for both executives and employees, especially as the challenges of private life and the challenges of work merge as never before.

What are the fundamental assumptions that employers and employees, staff members and volunteers, bring to the workplace? When inevitable changes, and radical negative and positive stresses, shake the business environment, who will guide the company with a steady hand and who will bail out in self-interest? Reasonable optimism must be grounded in a fundamental continuity of hope. Behind the moral collapse of recent corporate scandals lies an even deeper discontinuity between the faith stance of senior executives and the faith stance of other employees regarding the possibility of absolute justice or one's personal alignment with an ultimate purpose to life.

Motivating Vision

A motivating vision is the "song in the heart" that elicits incredible joy in the lives of organizational participants, shapes the rhythm of their work, and demands to be shared with strangers. The most common resistance to this simple statement is to assume that visions are the products of human ingenuity. If visions are simply created, then their primary value is in marketing. If visions are *revealed,* then their primary purpose is to claim the hearts and loyalties of followers and align them to a greater purpose.

The language of "visioning" is inherently religious. Visions come to individuals who are often at the fringe of the community and yearning for deeper purpose in life. They are shared as a team vision, become a community vision, and survive only as they are shared ever more inclusively with strangers. The most significant thing about visions as revealed is that they *hurt.* They always come in apocalyptic power to radically change or transform our lives. This is the reason "visioning processes" are generally resisted, and transformed instead into strategic planning processes. Visioning processes inevitably lead to pain as well as productivity. Strategic planning processes can change the world. Visioning processes change the leaders and members of an organization *on the way to changing the world.*

Servant-empowering organizations are more preoccupied with people than programs. Transform and align people to a larger purpose, and free them to invent the tactics to achieve it. Visioning processes, therefore, are inherently spiritual formation processes. They are really about building and shaping the character of leaders, members, and the organization as a whole. Strategic planning processes are simply task-prioritization processes. They ignore the character of leaders, and instead prescribe the incremental stages required to accomplish some program. Traditional organizations resist true visioning processes.

All religious organizations (Jewish, Christian, Muslim, and others) gravitate to visioning processes, but the more institutionalized they become, and the more distant they become from their original movements, the more they resist visioning processes. Leaders become convinced that they can discern a vision over a single weekend retreat with the trustees and announce it to the congregation on the next Holy Day. Visions actually require more time to develop. They emerge from the growing consensus about values and beliefs. It is not that the organization is just passively waiting for a vision, but that they are seeking, yearning, or questing for that vision. They position themselves to receive that vision, knowing full well that when it comes it will hurt. It will change them. Vision results from an earnest dialogue with infinite meaning.

All this may make sense of religious organizations, but does it apply to nonprofit, small business, and corporate organizations? In the emerging world, the answer is yes. All organizations are "faith-based" organizations whether or not their "faith" is in a God, the gods, a life force, science, or their own exaggerated abilities. Think about this. Study the origins of nonprofits, small businesses, and even successful corporations. The founders did not create a good idea; a great idea *seized* them. A higher, noble purpose captured their imagination and became a literal obsession. They did not start with a strategic plan. That came later. They started with an idea that many declared unreasonable, immoral, or just plain stupid. As the organization distanced itself from the original ecstasy and became more institutionally preoccupied with programs, products, and budget lines, it forgot its higher purpose, only to become ever more "machine-like." It became less willing to accept radical change. It drifted from its original purpose. Today nonprofit, small business, and corporate leaders are on a religious quest to regain the vision that was lost. That quest has more to do with the character of the corporate leaders than the products, structures, or financial management of the company.

Vision is not a statement or a plan. If you can say it all in words, or outline it all in an incremental timeline, you have missed the point. Visions are always beyond description. Words and plans are only a faint approximation, and yet the urgency, excitement, and passion are clearly displayed in the faces and behavior of organizational members. It is more like a song or a rhythm that organizational members find themselves humming unthinkingly, and yet their walk and work has adjusted itself to its cadence. The vision is the inner joy about going to work–the complete 180-degree opposite of the dread and drudgery that most employees associate with the office. It makes organizational members in any role, from the boardroom to the mail room, rejoice that the organization still exists and that they have one more day to invest in it.

A true vision generates its own marketing. That is to say, the organizational members are so excited or fulfilled by their participation in a larger vision that they cannot help but share it with others. It's not just that they think their product is the best product among the competition, but that their company or congregation is the best company or congregation among the competition. Their shared vision is the best vision in the world, and they are thrilled to have a share in the ownership of it, *and they are willing to make enormous sacrifices to bring the vision to fruition.*

Strategic Mission

A strategic mission is the single, measurable, audacious goal that deserves all the sacrifice and support of organizational members, captures the imagination of the public, and can be printed on the side of a bus. At first glance, the definitions of vision and mission seem to be the same. The vision, however, may be highly motivating but amorphous. The strategic mission statement (and it is a statement) identifies the key leverage point that accomplishes the vision. If the organization puts all its energy in *this* strategic move, the vision will have a cascading influence on everything else. A strategic mission is that single, measurable, audacious goal, the achievement of which will leverage all kinds of change.

Resistance to this simple statement of strategic mission comes from the misperception that the organization itself can and should be the target of its own mission. Despite the rhetoric of preaching and the propaganda of corporate advertising, the organization is primarily self-serving rather than other-serving. Its mission is to survive or to perpetuate itself, rather than to grow and expand new markets. The best way to refocus away from the public and toward the self is to so diffuse, obscure, or distort the mission that it can no longer be measurable. No measurability implies no accountability, and the organization can prioritize all its energies on itself with a clear conscience that it still has "good intentions" toward the world.

Visions are like dynamite, and mission statements define where to set the charges. Many established church organizations (and organizations in other sectors as well) have allowed the dynamite to get wet, or have packed it away in straw because it is too dangerous. They don't know where to set the charges even if they were motivated to do so, and without measurable leverage points to apply the vision to the world their mission is all sound and fury with little result. They may experience "mega" crowds, big explosions, and lots of dust, awesome sound effects, and plenty of media attention—but when all is said and done, the mountain blocking the path is still there.

Traditional organizations replace visions with strategic plans; and they replace short, pithy, powerful mission statements with long summaries of program options. The so-called "mission statement" of many churches is really several paragraphs or pages long, basically outlining their denominational heritage and program options for worship, education, care giving, and outreach. Servant-empowering organizations have taken the time for a deeper, character-building, spiritual journey that has ended in enthusiastic ownership of a shared vision. Their mission statement is a few words and an image. The image conveys the rigorous focus of the vision; the few words of the statement indicate exactly where they will detonate their dynamite.

Building the Foundation of Trust

In the last ten years of organizational consulting, I have learned by experience and observation that it takes an organization (church, nonprofit, business, health care provider, etc.) about three years to build the foundation of trust. Each year brings a further refinement and alignment of the core values, beliefs, vision, and mission of the organization. The first year this may involve a broad, consensus-building strategy across the organizational constituency using focus groups and interview teams in a process akin to what I first described in *Moving Off the Map*.[2] In the second year this may involve core leadership in retreat using a process akin to what I describe in the "Vision Retreat" tool offered through www.easumbandy.com.. In the third year this may be a dialogue between core leaders and outside mission partners and networks extending from the organization. There is nothing magic about three years. I have simply observed that the process cannot be artificially hurried even by the most passionate and focused leaders; and it should not be allowed to extend beyond three years by timid, tentative, or controlling organizational members.

The foundation of trust is only erected and maintained through personal pain, group sacrifice, and constant toil. Many organizations assume that simply gathering the bricks, mortar, and tools is sufficient. They sort out the core values, beliefs, vision, and mission into little piles on the ground; assemble the tools; and pin up a picture of how the finished structure should look. Then they all pray about it, celebrate it, drink champagne in a spirit of false harmony, and *think* they have a foundation of trust. In fact, they

---

[2]Ibid.

need to hammer those core values, beliefs, vision, and mission into the very souls and behaviors of their people. They need to spend three years–and more–toiling in the hot sun, arguing with each other, forgiving each other, and cooperating together to cement the bricks and mortar together into a solid, enduring foundation. Only then will the superficial harmony give way to a lasting trust.

The foundation of trust is hard work. Indeed, as we shall see later in the discussion of board and management responsibilities, the maintenance of that foundation of trust is the single most important task of leadership. The board will spend much of its time focusing on motivating vision and strategic mission. The management structure will spend most of its time articulating expectations of core values and bedrock beliefs. How is this done?

The foundation of trust is rigorously maintained in five ways. The details about board, management, and staff roles in maintaining the foundation of trust will be discussed later. Here I simply identify the key ways the foundation of trust is used to measure the focus and effectiveness of organizational life.

The Maintenance of Trust

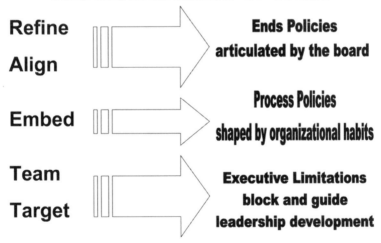

Refine **Align**	**Ends Policies** **articulated by the board**
Embed	**Process Policies** **shaped by organizational habits**
Team **Target**	**Executive Limitations** **block and guide** **leadership development**

As we shall see, the board and senior pastor (or CEO) take responsibility to focus the vision and mission of the organization and align all the pieces to deliver the mission *and nothing else.* The management teams and various staff take responsibility to ensure that every team functions within and articulates the core values, beliefs, vision, and mission of the organization. Management teams and staff customize the message for the cultural targets of the mission field and marketplace. All leaders model the values and beliefs in their lifestyles and hold all organizational members accountable for their behavior within and beyond the organization. Servant empowerment actually requires more rigor than the oversight exercised by traditional organizations, because work and lifestyle merge in the maintenance of trust.

These five ways to analyze the effectiveness of core values, beliefs, vision, and mission in shaping the activity and direction of the organization are applied to the five strategic areas of organizational life:

- Structure and mandates
- Funding and investment
- Training and staffing
- Communications and marketing
- Product development and research

Leaders continually ask: How effectively do each of these areas of organizational life regularly refine, align, embed, team up for, and target the mission of our organization? Any activity or deployment of energy, in any of these areas of organizational life, that does not perfectly align with the mission of the organization, is terminated. Any opportunity, in any of these areas of organizational life, that is not fully supported to align with the mission, is enhanced.

The hard work of maintaining the foundation of trust is best carried out "negatively." In other words, organizational leaders do not reflect abstractly about how the behavior of the organization should be, but they study concretely where the organization has failed. Such "negative thinking" helps focus leaders on the key places where mission goes awry and trust breaks down, and provides clues for the strategic moves that will refocus the mission and renew the trust.

Refining the Mission

Core values, beliefs, vision, and mission must be tested against the complexity and constant change of the mission field or marketplace. The board and senior staff take the lead in reviewing demographic and lifestyle trends, and prayerfully pondering the values, beliefs, vision, and mission of the organization. After the initial three years necessary to build the foundation of trust, the organization must continue to experience "movement" and "flexibility" as core values, beliefs, vision, and mission evolve. People grow. Spirit is dynamic. Contexts change. The role of senior leadership is to be so sensitive to these movements of culture and spirit that they can continually refine and adjust the values, beliefs, vision, and mission of the organization.

The best way to do this is to study "the margins." Who is left out? How does it feel to be left out? What is left undone? What is the impact of what is left undone on the rest of the productivity of the organization? Studying "the margins" is directly opposite to the habit of most traditional organizations. Their boards and senior leaders spend most of their time surveying the membership, listening to membership needs, and responding to membership concerns. The more frequent the worshiper, the better the giver, the greater the seniority, or the more needy the individual, the more attention they get. Servant-empowering organizations refine the mission by concentrating on the margins or edges, the people least involved who could become involved, and the issues unaddressed that need to be addressed. Witness the struggle of the Roman Catholic Church to acknowledge women in leadership.

Aligning with Mission

Mission units must be designed and leaders deployed to model the core values and beliefs of the organization, to pursue the vision of the organization, and to deliver the mission of the organization—and nothing else. The board and senior staff take the lead in reviewing the deployment of energy in the major pieces of the organization just as management and team leaders will review the deployment of energy in each sphere of their influence.

Over time, every organization accumulates programs and tactics that may become increasingly tangential to their original purpose, but which are perpetuated from habit. Every organization modifies programs and products in ways that no longer make sense for the purpose of the organization. The best way to align mission is to study these "sidetracks." Where do we waste the most time? What financial commitments bear the least fruit? When do leaders feel the most doubt? What plans seem to lead nowhere, and what products result in the least change? Again, studying the "sidetracks" is directly opposite to the habit of traditional organizations. They become so obsessed in perpetuating and micro-managing programs that they fail to evaluate whether they effectively deliver mission results anymore. Even the most "sacred" programs can become sidetracks over time. Witness the Salvation Army's obsession with nineteenth-century uniforms and brass bands.

Embedding the Mission

Core convictions, vision, and mission must be revealed in the daily routine of work and the actual lifestyles of organizational leaders and members. In the era of "professionalism" constructed by and for modernity, organizations sought to deliberately separate private life and work. Clergy became obsessed protecting "days off" and "vacation time." Nonprofit leaders got unlisted telephone numbers and refused to talk about work if they met a client on the sidewalk or in the supermarket. Corporate leaders and middle managers resented any expectation that the values of the workplace should be modeled at home—and that their continued employment would be staked on the continuity. The most stressful challenge to modern "professionalism" is the emergence of the small business and web-based entrepreneur who have left such artificial distinctions behind.

The best way to study how effectively values, beliefs, vision, and mission are embedded into personal lifestyle is to analyze the "failures." Team accountability is not only a critique of mistakes at work, but of mistakes in life. What didn't work? Who hindered, undermined, or blocked success? Where did the credibility break down? Where did we (and more personally, where did "I") fall short? The seamless credibility of personal lifestyle and effective mission makes sense for churches and nonprofits, but corporations have also become aware of the importance of lifestyle expectations for the harmony, risk-taking trust, research and development, and marketing success of the corporation. The "DNA" of the organizational body must be visibly modeled in the lifestyles of workers, or the organization loses consumer respect and partner trust. Witness the sexual abuse scandals that have accelerated Protestant and Catholic worship decline.

Teaming for Mission

To be radically creative, mission units must be trusted. They must constantly refer to values, beliefs, vision, and mission goals for constant accountability. In the modern era of "professionalism," all that really mattered was competence and the readiness to be trained. In the emerging world of constant adaptability, what really matters is a passionate sense of vocation and an absolute loyalty to the essential mission of the larger organization. Cooperation is everything. The only way to be competitive in the world is rigorously to *stop being competitive* within the organization. Non-cooperative mavericks, no matter how competent or brilliant, ultimately undermine the long-term viability of an organization.

The best way to study the effective "teaming" for mission is to analyze the "burnouts." Leaders burn out whenever team cooperation breaks down. Where is the biggest gap in volunteers? How do teams identify their level of incompetence? Who is exhausted (emotionally empty, creatively blocked, physically ill)? The more passionate and aligned leaders, who really merge work and lifestyle, bear more and more of the burden of productivity. The team itself may project an appearance of unity and mutual support, but team members sustain their energy at different levels. "Burnout" implies an inability to share work or an inability to assume work. Witness the staff co-dependencies that send so many mainstream church clergy to disability.

Targeting the Mission

Organizational leaders and mission units must focus on those partners and projects that can become "living proof" of the organization's values, beliefs, vision, and mission. The public observes the activities and networks of the organization as "natural": obviously compatible with the identity of the organization. Moreover, the organization must interpret or translate their mission into language or actions that a target microculture or public can understand.

The best way to study the effective targeting of mission is to analyze the "irrelevancies." Which mission partners do we ignore the most? Which mission partners ignore us the most? Which projects and publics receive the least resource, training, and support? Not all irrelevancies should become relevant. Perhaps these are "sidetracks" for organizational energy. Some "irrelevancies," however, reveal hidden addictions to self-interest. Witness the widening gap between many evangelical churches from the social service and health care sectors about which they claim to be concerned.

The analysis of "negative thinking" can be focused on each of the five key areas of organizational life. The appendix at the end of this book provides an example of how this is done. A positive outcome is stated in each of the five categories:

• Structure and mandates
• Funding and investment
• Training and staffing
• Communications and marketing
• Product development and research

Team members, organizational leaders, or mission partners can all "score" on a scale of 1–10 how effectively the organization approximates that outcome. Any score lower than 7 demands the attention of organizational leaders; any score lower than 5 suggests serious intervention is required; and any score lower than 3 strongly implies the necessity of firing leaders or terminating volunteers in the organization.

Conclusion

Over the past ten years of coaching churches, denominations, nonprofits, and businesses, I have found myself replacing the terminology of "rigorous adherence" to the DNA of the organization with the terminology of "ruthless adherence." Many are offended by the choice of words, and I have observed that the degree to which they are offended corresponds to the rapidity with which their organization is dying. Servant-empowering organizations do have a reputation for accepting, transforming, coaching, and deploying people who might otherwise be ignored by traditional organizations. The word *servant* is generally regarded as a "nice" word, and "ruthless" may seem inconsistent when used in the same context. Yet the whole point of a servant-empowering organization is to motivate and equip people *to serve something more important than themselves!* A servant is only a servant if the mission comes first.

However accepting, inclusive, generous, or encouraging organizational leaders might be, when it comes to refining, aligning, embedding, teaming, and targeting the mission they must be absolutely merciless. If they break down and exercise a false "mercifulness" to a single employee or team that is too beloved to discipline, there will be a cascading and destructive impact on the other team members, mission partners, and client publics who will inevitably be harmed by this relaxation of mission urgency. For every "beloved organizational member" who cannot be disciplined, numerous lifestyle segments are marginalized, precious resources are sidetracked, numerous colleagues burn out, countless organizational members assume it is OK to fail, and multiple mission partners are let down. Leaders can be flexible in all else, but they must be absolutely ruthless when it comes to adherence to the core values, bedrock beliefs, motivating vision, and strategic mission of the truly, fully, passionately, and urgently servant-empowering organization.

Boundary Thinking

The servant-empowering organization seeks to recover the original experience of a missional movement. Therefore, they approach accountability very differently than do traditional hierarchies and bureaucracies. Servant-empowering organizations say, "live within this…and avoid doing that"; traditional organizations say, "do all of this…and you shall be rewarded." Accountability in the latter organization is all about task performance and task supervision, with the promise of membership perks and future bonuses if you do the tasks in the prescribed manner, in the prescribed timetable, to the prescribed standard of quality. Accountability in a servant-empowering organization, however, is closer to the experience of the original movement from which organizational life evolved. Accountability is about staying within specific boundaries and proscribing specific actions.

Accountability

Accountability in a servant-empowering organization is designed to encourage creativity, ruthlessly align organizational activities with a higher missional purpose, and grow leaders. Accountability in a traditional organization is designed to encourage obedience, rigorously standardize with uniform processes, and maintain programs. The word *accountability* is often indiscriminately applied in both ways, and part of the challenge for organizational leaders is to sort these differences out. We are not just talking about different modes of accountability; we are not just comparing "apples" and "oranges." We are talking about two radically different styles of accountability, *which are essentially incompatible with one another;* it is more like comparing "fruit" and "vegetables." "Boundary thinking" and "task thinking" are two diametrically opposed ways of thinking.

Mission Movement or Institution

No better example of the difference between accountability in a missional movement and accountability in an institution (at least for a church audience) presents itself than the story of the exodus. How did the Israelites organize themselves to get to the promised land? They knew it would be a difficult and dangerous trek across a large desert, beset by many enemies, and with little food and water. Yet no story tells us how Moses managed the march; no charts of food and water rationing; and no instructions about what to do and when to do it. Instead, the organization of the missional movement looked like this:

- Miriam led the way singing. This was the vision, or the "song in the heart," that set the cadence for the march and pointed them in the right direction. Indefinably, but powerfully, they followed the pillar of smoke by day and the pillar of fire by night.
- Core convictions about being a chosen people, confidence in the rescuing power of God, and a freedom from oppression that was worth dying for were embedded in the hearts of the people.
- Moses declared: *Live with this!* You shall love the Lord your God with all your heart, and soul, and mind, and strength. This was the spirit of the covenant formed long ago with Abraham, Isaac, and Jacob.
- Moses went on to declare: *Do whatever you want, except...!* They could pitch their tents; engage in commerce; laugh, dance, and play any way they wanted, *but*...they could not kill, steal, fornicate, worship idols, abandon their parents, or cheat their neighbors. Just avoid doing those things, and they could do whatever else they wanted.
- Moses was ruthless in aligning the people to the mission. He was remarkably tolerant about all kinds of idiosyncratic behavior; remarkably encouraging for creative and innovative initiative; and absolutely terrifying when anybody stepped beyond those boundaries.

Sadly, it is all too easy to imagine how traditional organizations might have managed the exodus. No doubt they would have developed an incremental strategic plan; listed countless tasks to be done and procedures to be followed; appointed multiple layers of middle management to supervise everything; extended the journey through the wilderness another forty years to allow time for all the meetings; and justified it all with the glib conviction that, after all, what really was important was the quality of the journey rather than getting to the promised land.

Over time, the missional movement became an institution. The tasks, duties, and obligations multiplied. So also did the management structure, manual of procedures, and personnel guidelines. So also did the politics, manipulations, and lobbying by special interest groups. Jesus called the Israelites back to the original organizational principles of the missional movement. He redeveloped the fundamental "policies" within which the organization should live. In addition to a policy to "love God with all the heart," he added, "love your neighbor as yourself." "You can do anything," he said, "but you have to live with that." He then interpreted and restated the handful of executive limitations that members of the movement should avoid doing at all costs. Two thousand years later, the institutional church has essentially returned the organizational model to pre-Jesus times.

Although this is a specifically religious example, the same principles and challenges are true for the emergence of nonprofit and for-profit organizations. Most organizations began and developed as missional movements. Somebody was seized by a vision, focused a mission, shared it with a team, and started on a journey to a "promised land." The core values and beliefs may or may not have been explicit, but they were certainly inscribed on the hearts of the organizational members. The leader held the team ruthlessly to the vision, developed key policies to shape the habitual behavior of the organization, and identified a handful of action limitations. This encouraged creativity and initiative, allowing the nonprofit or for-profit to adapt to new contexts and expand into new markets.

Institutional Shifts

Then, as the missional movement "institutionalized," the positive outward momentum slowed, and the organization turned inward. Three shifts happened:

- *Guidelines became rules*: Organizational coaching that once provided options or suggestions now specifies exactly how things should be done. This usually happens because organizational growth has led to more complexity; and it is easier and more expedient for managers to control budgets, staff, and programs if processes are standardized.
- *Stories became heritages*: Organizational legend that was once used to describe core values and convictions, or inspire entrepreneurs in the spirit of the founders, now becomes sacred history that must be honored at all costs. This usually happens because unclear foundations of trust have made the organization vulnerable to competing ideologies, and the old stories must be reinterpreted to be politically correct.
- *Metaphors became blueprints*: Organizational comparisons, images, and examples that once stimulated creative imagination are now solidified into "the way things must be done around here." This usually happens because organizational leaders are more interested in career advancement than mission success.

In general, as a missional movement institutionalizes, "boundary thinking" is replaced by "task managing." Trust is replaced by oversight. Mission is replaced by maintenance. The organization is shaped around the convenience of management and the control of hierarchies rather than around effectiveness in achieving mission goals. The nonprofit or for-profit organization loses its way in the wilderness. They become so busy watching their step on the path that they miss the turnoff for the promised land. The servant-empowering organization intentionally reverses the institutionalizing process and returns the organization to its roots as a missional movement.

Defining Boundaries: Live within This...

The servant-empowering organization defines boundaries within which leaders and participants can do anything they want, but beyond which they cannot go. Defining, articulating, and training others to know and respect these boundaries is a primary function of senior staff (including senior pastor) and board. These "boundaries" may also be called "policies." Policies are neither more–nor less– than the corporate habits that are intentionally taught and trained within the organization.

These "policies" are the logical extension of the organizational consensus for core values, bedrock beliefs, motivating vision, and strategic mission. Policies help translate theory into praxis. Policies identify the repetitive, daring, and normative behavior patterns that distinguish one organization from another.

For example, the Roman Catholic Church believes in seven sacraments crucial for salvation. That is a bedrock belief. Therefore, they also believe that members should intentionally, regularly, and daringly participate in these sacraments, and that their priests cannot fail to offer these sacraments even at the risk of their own lives. That's a policy. A priest will risk his life on a battlefield pausing to give the "Last Rites" to a dying soldier. Others may think this unnecessary, foolhardy, and even reckless as a distraction to their own soldiers. Yet it is an expectation–a boundary–that is entirely consistent with the bedrock beliefs of the organization. If a priest were to fail in this expectation, he would be "outside the boundary" of Roman Catholic organizational life and held accountable.

Policies as Sacred

Priests might object that reference to the duty of a priest regarding the seven sacraments as a "policy" trivializes a practice God commanded. Yet this divine command has really been refined, focused, and interpreted by credible spiritual leaders of the church, and that is certainly a board function. Boards must be spiritual leaders precisely because they translate abstract belief into consistent, trainable behavior. The reality is that policies in any organization (even nonprofit and for-profit organizations) should be treated with the same respect as a "sacrament." That is to say, policies carry the weight of authority because they are the gateway between overarching missional purpose and daily organization practice.

The criticism of traditional bureaucracies and hierarchies is that they treat organizational policies as "sacred cows." The response is to do everything possible to ignore, avoid, work around, and generally mothball organizational policies to get work done. In fact, it is not the policies that are sacred in traditional organizations, but the controllers who interpret the policies. It is power, power politics, and intimidating or expertly manipulative individuals and factions that are truly "sacred" to the traditional organization. Traditional organizations operate like a state in which what is truly sacred is the officeholder, not the law. Would that policies *were* sacred to the organization!

Policies over Power

The servant-empowering organization can allow enormous freedom, creativity, and innovation precisely *because* they take their policies so seriously. "Policy" takes precedence over "power." This is why innovative participants in a servant-empowering organization do not need to obtain permission from a hierarchy, a patriarch, or committee to take initiative. The "policies" are immediately transparent to any and all participants as "boundaries" for behavior, and so long as one stays within these policies, permission is already granted to take initiative. So what if it offends "very powerful people"? They are powerless before policy. Their personal tastes, political preferences, or family needs are irrelevant. Policies in the servant-empowering organization do have a "sacramental" nature; and therefore policymakers (the board and senior staff) must be spiritually credible people. The board of a nonprofit or for-profit organization has a spiritual character, because they are the guardians of the boundaries.

What exactly does a "policy" look like? This question will be explored in more detail as we discuss the proper function of a board. The principle of "boundary thinking," however, means that policies are not programs or tactics. They do not identify any particular task as "sacred." They do identify particular "habits" as sacred.

For example, imagine the well-trained property manager of a servant-empowering Methodist Church looking at a wall scheduled for demolition. She asks herself: "Is the demolition of this wall going to better align our organization to achieve its mission?" She then reflects on what is known among Methodists as the "Wesleyan Quadrilateral." This may be done intentionally or unthinkingly, but as she frowns broodingly at the wall you are reasonably confident what is going on in her head. She is reflecting on the *history* of her church (i.e., the radical pragmatism of the Wesleyan movement that generally shunned property ownership in general); the *theology* of her church (i.e., the conviction that connecting sinful people with sanctifying grace was all-important); the *reasonableness* of the plan (i.e., removing the wall will make more space for worshiping people); and the *spirit* of the decision (i.e., trusted spiritual leaders think God wants this done now). The corporate habit of the Wesleyan Quadrilateral used in all problem solving is the policy of the church. Having satisfied herself that she is within the boundaries of the organization, and knowing full well that demolishing the wall will offend a dozen people, she gives the order: *"Tear down the wall!"*

Now compare this decision to that of a well-trained property manager of a servant-empowering Reformed Church. He, too, is looking at a wall scheduled for demolition. He asks himself: "Is the demolition of this wall going to better align our organization to achieve its mission?" He sees that the wall has inscribed upon it inspiring words from the Heidelberg Confession. He remembers that the wall belongs to the original construction by saintly pilgrims in 1747. He knows that the mission of the church demands more room for worship. The corporate habit of the Reformed Church is to honor the past and educate people in the original principles of the Reformation. Having considered the boundaries of organizational life, and knowing full well that keeping the wall will offend a dozen people, he gives the order: *"Tear down the rest of the building, but at all costs preserve this wall!"*

The example illustrates how policies are more important than power brokers. Policies may be focused and articulated by a board, but they are transparent to every participant in the organization. They are rigorously trained and constantly refreshed in the minds of leaders and members. They allow radical initiatives to be rapidly implemented, without inviting unnecessary conflict. Outside observers may or may not agree with the decision to tear down or preserve a wall, but they must be able to clearly see and respect the continuity of the decision with the policies of the organization. In both the Methodist and Reformed church examples, we can easily imagine "Historic Preservation Societies" and other special interest groups lobbying the church to make a particular decision. Churches that are unclear about their policies will succumb to the most powerful lobby or become bogged down in endless meetings. Churches that are clear about their policies *will not really care about the lobbying groups.* They will make decisions that align *their own* organizational mission, rather than decisions that align their property to someone else's organizational mission.

The Fewer Policies the Better

The servant-empowering organization does not need many policies; the fewer the better. As the organization grows, the ratio of policies to people and program *grows larger.* Even with a huge diversity of people and many different programs, the actual number of policies should remain relatively small. This means that policies must be made with extreme care. They should aim at strategic leverage points in the life of the organization. The best policy is one that, if adhered to rigorously, will subsequently, automatically, align a myriad of other programs and projects to the mission of the organization. The larger the organization becomes, the more intentional and careful they must become in developing policy; the more deliberate and regular they must become in refining policy; and the more assertive and ruthless they must become in communicating and training policy.

Obviously, the definition of "policy" for a servant-empowering organization is different from the definition of "policy" for a traditional organization. We are not talking about tasks that need to be done, but about the way all tasks need to be approached. These are the handful of carefully selected and crafted organizational habits that all members of the organization must live within. A significant role of senior staff and board is to protect the essential spirituality, integrity, and purposefulness of the organization.

   a. *Spirituality:* When organizations simply list what can or should be done, they limit the power of the Holy Spirit to interrupt the strategic plan and carry organizational energy in new directions. However, when organizations concentrate on broad policies that shape the organizational way of life, activities can flow in unexpected directions from the spiritual formation discipline of the participants.

   b. *Integrity:* When organizations simply make lists of activities or programs that they feel obliged to implement, they limit the imaginations of the participants and distance members from their own sense of personal destiny. However, when organizations concentrate on setting clear boundaries for values, beliefs, vision, and mission, they anchor participants in the meaning of their personal and shared daily relationships with God, and motivate any corporate activity by a quest for personal fulfillment.

   c. *Purposefulness:* When organizations simply describe a denominational or local heritage that they wish to protect, they limit the potential for good that lies within the corporate body for God's world. However, when organizations concentrate on clarifying the unique calling and passion shared by participants, they focus enormous and constant energy for positive change to the neighborhood and the world.

The clearer an organization is about its policies, the more readily the organization can ruthlessly adhere to the core values, bedrock beliefs, motivating vision, and strategic mission of the organization. They can refine, align, embed, team, and target all aspects of the organization to pursue the vision and deliver the mission...*and nothing else.* New members will not dilute organizational integrity and spirituality; outside special interests will not sidetrack the organization from its clearly defined mission.

Defining Boundaries: Avoid Doing That...

The second aspect of "boundary thinking" is management by *pro*scription. We have already observed that a form of "negative thinking" is most useful to refine, align, embed, team, and target the mission of an organization. This same principle can be extended to help managers hold various organizational leaders and members accountable for their actions even in the midst of radical and chaotic innovation. "Proscription" is what Moses practiced using the "Ten Commandments," each of which begins with the words, "Thou shalt not..." It is what the Jerusalem Council practiced (Acts 15) in resolving the dispute with Paul over the mission to the Gentiles. Any missionary tactic was acceptable, they said, so long as new Christians refrained from a handful of specific things. "*Pro*scription" is the pragmatic management tool of any missional movement.

Not Permission-giving Management

This is why the terminology of "permission-giving" is not really accurate to describe the servant-empowering organization. The terminology implies that innovative leaders and teams first need to explain their particular initiative (the design, implementation strategy, and evaluation template) to management, and management will be predisposed to "give permission" if it is within the boundaries or policies of the organization. Yet this very necessity of explaining initiatives to management should be avoided if the organization is to be rapidly adaptive, utterly creative, and encouraging toward innovators. What creative leader wants to stand in line for the attention of management, even if they are said to be predisposed to "give permission"? If they are really "permission-giving," why bother to explain it to them the first place? The fist within the glove is that "permission-giving" management obviously has the option of being "permission-withholding" management, and the charade about predisposition simply camouflages the same old hierarchy.

In a truly servant-empowering organization, management does not care what leaders and teams do. They don't want to hear about it. They don't want to read reports about it. They neither give nor withhold permission to do anything. They do not function as an "approval" body. Management *does care* what leaders and teams *do not do*. They *cannot* go beyond the boundaries or policies of the organization. To protect those boundaries, management will identify key, strategic, executive limitations on the actions of teams and leaders. They can do anything, *but they cannot do* these *things*.

A Change in Accountability

This changes the entire experience of accountability. Management does not waste time listening to what leaders and teams are doing. They do not need to know, and if creativity is really blossoming in the organizational mission they do not have time to know. Instead, the experience of accountability is a reality check that teams and leaders are *not* doing specific things they were told not to do. We will explore what various kinds of "*pro*scriptions" might look like later in this book. The point here, however, is that *this* kind of negative thinking is actually more freeing, encouraging, and empowering to innovation and initiative than long task lists and requirements.

The most obvious example is that managers tell team leaders that the leaders may hire and fire whomever they please (so long as the hiring and firing aligns with and maximizes the mission of the organization), but leaders *cannot fail* to keep up to date on evolving federal and state human rights legislation. Protective laws regarding the hiring or firing of disabled persons, for example, have changed repeatedly over the past ten years. Although such a proscription seems obvious, it is remarkable how often churches, nonprofits, and even corporations do not have such a proscriptive policy and fail to protect the rights of disabled persons. Most litigation against churches has nothing to do with theological, liturgical, or evangelistic practices that are consistent with their values, beliefs, vision, and mission. They have to do with specific failures or breakdowns in trust. The managers of the church were so busy reading reports to make sure that voluminous lists of tasks were accomplished, that they failed to protect the organization from specific lapses, failures, and abuses in which leaders went beyond the boundaries.

Executive Limitations: Curbing the Willfulness of Leaders

Another way to speak of "proscriptive policies" is to describe "executive limitations." The board mandates management to do whatever is necessary to align the organization to mission and to maintain the boundaries of core values and beliefs. The board then proscriptively identifies selected limitations on their actions. So long as they do not violate these limitations, the board can be free to do the visioning, research, prayer, and other decision-making that will position the organization to be relevant in the long term. However, they will check with management to make sure they have not done anything they were expressly told not to do. The same principle is repeated as management works with any and all teams that are doing various pieces of work for the organization.

If you were reading carefully, you will have noticed a key item in the above example of proscriptive thinking. Leaders can do whatever is necessary, excepting only specific executive limitations on their actions, *so long as their decisions align with and maximize the mission of the organization.* Once again, ruthless alignment with the mission is revealed as a key factor of accountability in the servant-empowering organization. Many leaders are under the mistaken impression that to be "empowered" as a "servant" means being allowed to do whatever they want to do. The complete opposite is in fact the case. The "servants" are defined by their relationship to a "master," or, in this case, by their surrender to a clearly defined, higher purpose. Leaders are servants when they surrender their work and lifestyles to a specific vision or mission.

Therefore, to empower servants, managers must curb the "willfulness" of leaders. This is done, not by prescribing long lists of tasks and procedures, but by making sure that the actions of leaders are aligned to deliver the mission of the organization…*and nothing else.* Once again, we see a form of "negative thinking" at the heart of the organization. Management aligns the organization to mission by saying in effect: "Not this, not this, not this, not this…but *this!*" It is obvious, I think, that such management decisions are both quantitative and qualitative. That is to say, alignment to mission can be measured quantitatively. Church leaders, for example, might define the following *pro*scriptive policy:

No worship service will be continued if the percentage of visitors to members drops below 25%.

This prevents the perpetuation of worship services on which the resources of the church are expended that serve only a small minority of inward-looking members, and do not encourage inclusive outreach. On the other hand, church leaders might continue a small-attendance healing worship service, for example, that has a qualitative impact on the hospitals and clinics that surround the neighborhood in that particular urban community. It's a "judgment call," and therefore it requires high trust and spiritual credibility on the part of the leaders.

Executive limitations only make sense in the context of ruthless alignment with mission. If there is no ruthless alignment with mission, then executive limitations appear to be merely arbitrary. Decisions are made based on personal perspective, allegiance to a powerful faction, or simply on the whim of controlling leaders. It is not really possible to manage a servant-empowering organization based on boundary thinking, unless somebody (a board) has the sole purpose to refine and align the organization to its mission. Only then can they reasonably delegate management to a trusted, gifted few and expect to practice accountability through *pro*scriptive thinking.

Separating Board and Management Function

The principles of boundary thinking require a separation of board function and management function. Again, this contrasts with traditional hierarchies and bureaucracies, which generally conflate the two functions. In traditional organizations, boards find themselves drawn constantly into micro-management and spend little time on visioning. They cannot "let go control" enough for managers to lead through executive limitations. They must tell them what to do and how to do it. Boundary thinking requires that a board remain aloof from management so that they can devote time and energy to the refinement and alignment of vision and mission. Only then can management and the teams they manage have "reasonable trust" to be as creative and innovative as possible.

Size Makes No Difference in Philosophy

These principles hold true regardless of the size of the organization. Larger churches, nonprofits, businesses, and other organizations will have very small boards. Salaried staff with the expertise required for the job will fill the key management positions. An executive limitation might well be that the *human resources staff person* cannot fail to update himself or herself on evolving human rights legislation affecting the hiring and firing of other staff. Small churches and other small organizations will still have very small boards, but volunteers (or volunteer teams) will fill the key management positions. The principle of "servant empowerment" requires that these volunteers receive serious training in the core values, beliefs, vision, and mission of the organization; in the design and support of teams; and in the select policies and executive limitations refined by the board.

Nevertheless, even the smallest organizations will have a leader with a mission attitude. This leader will gather around himself or herself a small core group of like-hearted people (the beginnings of a "board") and will trust others to design, implement, and evaluate various ministries (the beginnings of true "teams"). These ministry or team leaders, in turn, will be informally coordinated and aligned by boundary-thinking leaders (the beginnings of servant-empowering "management"). The founder, owner, or pastor may start out by being totally involved in both visioning and management; but as the organization grows, he or she cannot maintain that involvement in both. If he or she stays immersed in management, the organization will evolve into traditional hierarchy or bureaucracy. If he or she "lets go" of management to focus on visioning, the organization evolves to be servant empowering or eventually plateaus in growth or disintegrates.

Even the smallest organizations (initial "church plants" and "entrepreneurial partnerships") should informally reflect the principles of the servant-empowering organization. Their leaders need to be trained to anticipate a servant-empowering organization, because if they are not trained in this way, they will almost certainly fall victim to the traditional organizational habits of modernity. The small church plant or entrepreneurial partnership will grow in membership, leadership, and mission impact. Quite uncritically and compulsively, it will suddenly birth committees, hierarchies, and bureaucracies. The legacy (or addictions) of 300 years of modernity cannot be overcome without intentional training.

Yet the organization faces an urgent need to overcome the organizational addictions of modernity. The paradox that challenges us today is that things are changing constantly, only to remain the same. On the one hand, we see a blur of change so rapid that traditional organizations cannot keep up; on the other hand, a singular lack of real creativity results from all that change so that progress remains essentially frozen. Unable to change rapidly and unable to encourage radical creativity, traditional organizations become increasingly irrelevant.

The Servant-empowering Difference

Servant-empowering organizations are different.

a. *Speed:* When organizations mandate staff and teams with prescriptive task lists, original and creative ideas are exceptions that require additional bureaucracy to approve. This takes time, which the rapidly changing mission field will not allow. However, when organizations mandate staff and teams with *pro*scriptive executive limitations, mission leaders are free to experiment without waiting for bureaucrats to catch up.

b. *Creativity:* When organizations write *pre*scriptive task lists, creativity is really measured by the group imagination of a controlling board. Before anything original can be tried, the board must be persuaded that it is possible. However, when organizations use *pro*scriptive mandates, mission leaders with creative ideas need only demonstrate that an experiment is *permissible* within the boundaries of congregational life. Whether the proposal is possible or not is limited only by the imagination of the mission leader.

c. *Relevance:* When organizations use *pre*scriptive task lists, the congregation becomes bound to a strategic plan that is not easily changed. The surrounding culture will change quickly, but the church is still committed to implement an explicit list of activities that are rapidly becoming irrelevant. However, when organizations use *pro*scriptive executive limitations, the congregation is committed to a *way of life,* but not to any detailed *strategic plan.* Mission leaders rapidly adjust ministries to the changing cultural environment.

The more an organization focuses boundaries and guides leaders through executive limitations, the more adaptable, innovative, and relevant they can become.

Conclusion

"Boundary thinking" is really more of a philosophy than a technology. It is a way of thinking, of approaching organizational challenges and opportunities, and of maintaining accountability. The opposite of "boundary thinking" is "task listing." This contrast, however, reveals a deeper significance to the servant-empowering organization. The philosophy of "task listing" means that the primary purpose of an organization is program development. The philosophy of "boundary thinking" means that the primary purpose of an organization is leader development. The organizations of modernity (oriented as they were to assembly lines, franchising, and unions) did business by first developing a program and then recruiting leaders to implement them. The organizations of postmodernity (oriented as they are to Web sites, entrepreneurship, and networks) do business by first growing and training leaders and then turning them loose to innovate programs.

Policy Governance

At first glance, the concept of policy governance seems anything but radical. In what other way can you run an organization? Yet most modern organizations have not really been governed by policy. They have been governed by personality, profit, and appeasement. The pressure for policy governance actually meets surprising resistance from both the "Builder" and "Boomer" generations and their legacies. The iconic industrial tycoons of the late nineteenth and early twentieth centuries did not govern by policy. The social service and church leaders who modeled themselves after such leadership grew industrial unions and denominations. The iconic post-war entrepreneurs of the late twentieth century did not govern by policy. The social service and church leaders who modeled themselves after *these* leaders grew charitable agencies and mega-churches. To understand the radical nature of policy governance, we need to understand the alternative.

Alternatives to Policy Governance

Governance by personality places responsibility for organizational development on the dominant presence of a leader. Organizational success is simply an extension of personal success. The president or CEO, pastor or executive secretary, basically "makes it up" as he or she goes. Everything depends on personal intuition to anticipate opportunities and on the force of their intimidating or inspiring presence to motivate implementation. Such personalities bestow authority to subordinates who share their personality and embrace their strategic plans. If the organization fails, in whole or in part, the organization replaces the leader. Patronage is always more important than policy.

Governance by profit subjects organizational development to the exigencies of financial crisis and entrepreneurial opportunity. The measurement of success is reduced to the size of the profit margin, which forces organizational thinking to be increasingly myopic and short-term. "Profit" may be described in other ways than mere dollars and cents, but the measurements of membership growth, property and technology expansion, staff and employee salaries, and mission influence ultimately boil down to the same thing. Decisions are based primarily on profitability. It is about institutional success that surpasses or outdistances the competition.

Governance by appeasement guides organizational development along the lines of least resistance. It may not be the happiness or internal harmony of the organization that matters, but simply the desire to lessen the degree of hassle in getting anything done. Do whatever is easier. Avoid confrontations, even if those confrontations might ultimately be productive. Make sure that all departments work together without misunderstandings or disagreements. The organization is predisposed to ignore personnel reviews and lower expectations for productivity and accountability, if in doing so the organization can run more smoothly.

In fact, modern organizations are constantly setting aside policy to exalt personalities, maximize profits, and preserve internal harmony. Much of the conflict experienced by organizations arises by an imbalance of these three things, and most of the solutions offered by consultants are designed to recover that balance. Yet nothing radically changes.

No clearer example of this resistance to policy governance offers itself than the United Methodist Church. The Methodist *movement* spread as a process of mentoring spiritually deep "amateurs" to use any means of transportation and housing that worked to travel the frontier and found cell groups. They intuitively followed a form of policy governance. As the movement crystallized into a denomination, however, the real functioning of the denomination, in all of its judicatories and councils, has become preoccupied with what one district superintendent sadly described as the "3 A's: Appointment, Apportionment, and Appeasement." Most of the time, energy, and budget of the institution are spent fixing and collecting the required financial contributions of the churches ("apportionments"), which fund the guaranteed salaries of the clergy ("appointments"). And the success of increasing apportionments and guaranteeing appointments largely depends on the happiness and harmony of the congregations ("appeasement"). United Methodist leaders find themselves doing what their nineteenth- and twentieth-century business counterparts did. They rely on strong personalities to give patronage to favored protégés, measure the profit margin between institutional maintenance and mission, and deploy therapeutic administrators to maintain the harmony of the financial base.

Of course, this is only one example among many. It illustrates what happens when a movement becomes an institution, which is the fate of all denominations of any brand name today and of all business and nonprofit organizations carrying legacies from the nineteenth and twentieth centuries. As I suggested in the previous chapter, the opposite of policy governance is task supervision. A direct correlation exists between policy governance and the reduction of bureaucracy, and between resistance to policy governance and the growth of bureaucracy. Expanded or complicated bureaucracy is the telltale sign that the organization does *not* govern itself by policy. It governs itself through personality, profit, and appeasement–and therefore guarantees the eventual irrelevance and obsolescence of the organization as leaders change, resource and development stagnates, and imagination is curtailed.

The Nature of Policies

Policies do not exist as individual statements, but as a chain of expectation that links accountability and productivity. One end of the chain is anchored in the core values, beliefs, vision, and mission of the organization … and the other end of the chain is anchored in a clear understanding of the market, culture, or mission field that the organization is designed to reach. Therefore, the servant-empowering organization is highly selective about its policies. Not just any policy will do. The policy that works well in one organization may not work in another, because the identity and the mission market will be slightly different. An appropriate policy is one that maximizes the connection between organizational purpose and organizational market. There are three links in the chain.

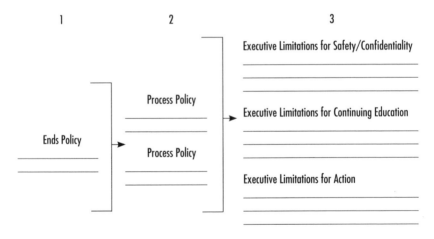

Organizational leaders begin with a clear understanding of their identity and vision–and a clear understanding of the mission and market. They then forge the links in the chain that will take them from accountability to productivity.

Ends Policies…

An "ends policy" is an "anticipated outcome." It extrapolates from the identity of the organization the expected result of the organization's existence. It does this in a way that organizational leaders can reasonably measure, either by quantifiable analysis or reasonable synthesis. An "ends policy" defines this result as either personal or social change.

This may lead some to assume that I am only talking about churches or nonprofit organizations, but exactly the same principle must be true for corporate, for-profit, and government organizations. An "ends policy" is *not* about profit margins, just as it is *not* about membership growth or property development or theological principle. It is plainly and simply a clear statement of what impact the existence of the organization will have on the mission market that the organization wishes to reach. Whenever change occurs, an opportunity arises for quantifiable financial, membership, and programmatic growth. The mere desire to make money, add members, or multiply programs, however, does not define the reason for existence of any organization. Wishful thinking does not precipitate opportunity; *personal and social change* precipitates opportunity. Regardless of the profit or nonprofit status of an organization, the most fundamental question that must be answered is how that organization should impact and change the market or mission field. That is an "ends policy."

An appropriate "ends policy" not only articulates the point of organizational life, but provides the means for evaluating success. For example:

- "Seekers and people with no Christian memory will experience spiritual coaching that will help them shape their personal relationships, career paths, and lifestyles around their relationship with Jesus Christ."
- "Parents (couples or singles) will become disciplined in spiritual growth and be equipped to communicate basic values and beliefs to their children at home."
- "Addicted people of all ages and backgrounds will awaken to their self-destructive habits, practice disciplines for personal and spiritual recovery, and form relationships to recover full health."
- "Homeless, friendless people will live in safety and learn to support each other in trusting relationships."
- "Volunteers motivated and informed by our values, beliefs, vision, and mission will be leaders on the governing boards of charitable organizations, boards of education, hospital boards, and municipal government in our community."
- "Business and government leaders in our neighborhood and municipality will receive regularly updated information and reliable coaching about safe environmental practices and sound environmental policies free of charge."
- "Business leaders will be able to share information, in every media, instantly, from any place on earth, no matter how remote."
- "Infectious diseases will be eliminated or readily contained by any national government committed to do so, regardless of wealth."

- "City dwellers will have safe, cheap, environmentally friendly, and readily available options for transportation that will enhance their diverse lifestyles."

Such an "ends policy" may define the overall point of the organization, or the point of a particular division, ministry, or activity of that organization. Even the most complex, multinational organizations really have only one "ends policy" for the entire organization. It is the unifying purpose or activity for all the various divisions and components of the organization. The organization may acquire other organizations that align with that policy or split off organizational units that do not align with that policy.

Therefore, each major division or ministry of the organization will similarly have such an "ends policy." It will clearly connect with the stated purpose of the organization, or enhance the purpose of the organization. The servant-empowering organization most naturally uses the metaphor of "organism." The organism is one body, with multiple and interdependent systems. It is one organization, with several key functions.

For example, it is common today to understand a faith community as being composed of five basic sub-systems. The overall purpose of congregational existence is described through five core processes, each of which has its own interrelated "ends policy." If the overall policy of the organization is that *"seekers and people with no Christian memory will experience spiritual coaching that will help them shape their personal relationships, career paths, and lifestyles around their relationship with Jesus Christ,"* then the major functions of congregational life may be focused as follows:

- *Change People:* Lives will be transformed (attitudes, relationships, commitments, careers, and priorities) in both comfortable and explainable, and uncomfortable and unexplainable, ways.
- *Grow Believers:* Faith will be deepened (conviction, understanding, and behavioral expectations) to equip people in sharing faith and coping with life struggles.
- *Discern Call:* Believers will discover personal mission and fulfill their lives joyously helping others in God's service.
- *Equip Leaders:* Passionate people will be trained in whatever skills they require, to do whatever mission they are called to do, at standards of quality equivalent or superior to the best examples in the community.
- *Deploy Servants:* Leaders will be empowered to change lives with all of the financial, technological, and property resources at our disposal.

These are all "ends policies" that collectively help the entire congregation achieve its anticipated outcome. They connect the DNA of the organization with the mission market of the organization. A similar definition of "ends policy" can be developed for any organization in any employment sector.

Process Policies...

Great care must be taken to differentiate the "process policies" of a servant-empowering organization from the "procedural requirements" of a traditional organization. A process policy is developed only in an atmosphere of high trust that has been established through clear consensus about core values, beliefs, vision, and mission—and in alignment with a simple, clear "ends policy" for the organization or primary unit of mission. In such an atmosphere, required procedures are unnecessary. Organizational habits are everything.

A "process policy" articulates an organizational habit. These habits do not really require a defined method of implementation and can be flexibly interpreted and applied by the leaders and members of an organization. Yet they are *habits* that are trained and engrained into the automatic behavior of staff and volunteers. They are as natural as breathing to organizational insiders, but they feel foreign to organizational newcomers. These organizational "habits," more than anything else, shape what becomes the "corporate culture" of the organization.

For example, an organizational outsider observes that every leader, member, or employee of a particular organization wears a suit coat or some form of jacket. The usual color is white. Personally, the observer prefers never wearing a suit coat or jacket and avoids white because it shows the dirt and requires too much maintenance. Yet the clear organizational "habit" is that volunteers and employees automatically wear white overcoats. If that observer is to become a part of the organization, he or she will have to acquire this new habit. They will have to learn that staff and volunteers wear jackets to multiply pockets, which help them carry all of the stethoscopes, thermometers, and other equipment they require to meet the unpredictable and urgent needs of their work. They will have to learn that the jackets are white to specifically show any dirt, since cleanliness is important in avoiding contamination. These "habits," in turn, align with the basic "process policy" of the clinic that "every employee and volunteer shall portably carry essential equipment to respond instantly and immediately to unexpected crises, and practice exceptionally high standards of cleanliness." A newcomer who is unable or unwilling to acquire this organizational habit will be dismissed from the organization.

Note in the example above that these are habits, not procedures. No memo demands that every employee launder their white coats on Monday mornings, prescribes a time when volunteers must show up for inspection, or provides forms that specify for some distant bureaucrat the actual number of pockets in one's jacket and how many centimeters wide they are. *Procedures* are mysterious requirements that must be scrutinized by authorized experts. *Habits* are transparent behavior patterns for which even the lowliest volunteer or employee can hold anyone accountable.

Obviously, few of these organizational habits need to be defined. The definition is important primarily for the training or enculturation of new volunteers and staff, although it is also important to maintain trust and integrity throughout the organization as its volunteers and employees become embroiled in the mission market. The faster newcomers are assimilated into an organization, the more the organizational identity can be diluted or distorted by habits that are distinct from, and even hostile to, the organization. The more an organization relevantly engages its mission market, the more the members of the organization are influenced by habits that are foreign to the organization.

An appropriate "process policy" identifies an organizational habit that is intrinsically connected to the core values, beliefs, vision, and mission of the organization—and that enhances or facilitates the "ends policy" of the organization or mission unit. For example:

- "The sacraments must be offered in all experiences of worship (regardless of style, size, or location), and to all people (regardless of membership, age, mental competence, or emotional maturity)."
- "All ideas and initiatives must be considered in reference to Scripture, the tradition of the ancient church, sound reasoning, and openness to the fresh presence of the Holy Spirit."
- "The daily routine must be punctuated by three occasions of deliberate, focused prayer, regardless of the task being performed or the context of life."
- "All employees and volunteers will model physical and mental fitness to the public at work and at leisure, and be invariably polite regardless of provocation."
- "Electronic communication will be the normal method of networking, and face-to-face meetings will rarely take longer than ten minutes."
- "Every volunteer and employee will be familiar with (and conversant in) the basic stories, teachings, miracles, and lifestyle advice of the Bible."
- "The leaders of any division or ministry will be in constant contact and conversation (24/7) with the leaders of every other division or ministry."

These organizational habits are deliberately not tied to any particular procedure or tactic. They leave considerable freedom to adapt these habits to one's own lifestyle, peculiar task, or specialized purpose. Yet these habits pervade the organizational culture and are deliberately taught to newcomers.

Just as servant-empowering organizations must make sure that "ends policies" are measurable expectations rather than wishful thinking, so also they must be careful to make their "process policies" clearly identifiable habits and not just good intentions. Avoid vague references to "being faithful," or qualified injunctions to "*try, seek, quest for, or pursue*" specific standards of behavior. Be clear: *faithful to what?* Be assertive: *do it, achieve it, and accomplish it.* If volunteers or employees fail to model the organizational habit, they are held accountable. They are held accountable not simply by leaders, but by every other member of the organization. Good intentions sabotage the integrity of the organization, but, more significantly, they break the policy chain that links organizational identity to the mission market. Loss of credibility leads to diminished impact.

Executive Limitations...

So far, the basic boundaries of core values, beliefs, vision, and mission (foundation of trust) of the organization have been refined and aligned by the positive articulation of ends policies and process policies. The third link in the chain between organizational identity and mission market is developed *proscriptively.* This is the decisive point where the servant-empowering organization turns away from traditional forms of governance.

In the midst of organizational consultation among traditional churches and nonprofit organizations, I can literally feel the impatience and eagerness of leaders who do not yet understand the radical nature of the servant-empowering organization. They have waited patiently (and perhaps condescendingly) during the explanation of "ends policies" because the personalities of these leaders are decidedly aggressive and "results driven." They have grown restless during the explanation of "process policies" because they sense that their power to control the organization through patronage appointments has weakened. They are surprised that we have not mentioned financial, membership, or programmatic "profits." Now they are they are muttering to themselves: "OK, when do I get to tell the employees and volunteers what to do?" It will come as a shock to hear the clear answer: "Never!"

Servant-empowering leaders never tell volunteers or employees what to do. They align volunteers and employees to a vision, define clear boundaries beyond which they cannot go, and articulate clear proscriptions that identify specific things they may not do. This last, rather negative sounding policy is called an "executive limitation." In the limitless array of strategies and tactics that could accomplish the mission, executive limitations select a handful of key strategies or tactics that are *not* permissible. This is the way the archetypal servant-empowering leader, Moses, led the children of Israel to the promised land. He clarified the "ends policy" and the "process policies," and then identified ten things the children of Israel could not do.

Moses started with the foundation of trust of the original covenant with Abraham, Isaac, and Jacob. It was based on brotherhood, not birthrights (core value); God's loving power, not the whims of the gods (bedrock belief); a vision of a heavenly ladder (God's real presence with the people); and a mission to be a blessing to the peoples on earth (the fruit of their relationship). Within that framework, Moses worked out the organizational principles of Israel:

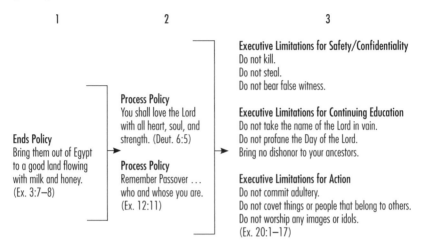

1	2	3
		Executive Limitations for Safety/Confidentiality Do not kill. Do not steal. Do not bear false witness.
	Process Policy You shall love the Lord with all heart, soul, and strength. (Deut. 6:5)	**Executive Limitations for Continuing Education** Do not take the name of the Lord in vain. Do not profane the Day of the Lord. Bring no dishonor to your ancestors.
Ends Policy Bring them out of Egypt to a good land flowing with milk and honey. (Ex. 3:7–8)	**Process Policy** Remember Passover . . . who and whose you are. (Ex. 12:11)	**Executive Limitations for Action** Do not commit adultery. Do not covet things or people that belong to others. Do not worship any images or idols. (Ex. 20:1–17)

This chain of policymaking linked the organizational identity of the people of Israel with their mission destination in the promised land. Interestingly, as the people of Israel evolved from movement to institution, they did exactly what Moses warned them not to do. They created more and more prescriptive rules, told the people what to do in micro-management, and essentially elevated sacred tasks and rituals into idols. God then sent a series of prophets, from Elijah to Jesus, calling them back to their servant-empowering roots.

Executive limitations "block and guide," using barriers that block behavior in order to guide volunteers and employees in the right direction. There are essentially three kinds of executive limitations. These are the key areas in which carefully selected "blocks" will force volunteers and staff members to align with the stated mission of the organization.

SAFETY AND CONFIDENTIALITY

The organization must protect the safety and confidentiality of its own people as well as the people who are a part of the mission market. This is an obvious necessity to protect the organization from litigation. In fact, designing an organization around policy governance (rather than personality, profit, or appeasement) is welcomed by the court because it is easier to monitor and measure risk. Traditional organizations tell people what to do and then have to monitor every activity and supervise every task to make sure people do it. The resulting bureaucracy is so cumbersome that it is easy for illegal or immoral actions to occur intentionally or unintentionally, and often very difficult to discover what went wrong, with whom, and where. Servant-empowering organizations selectively and carefully identify key proscriptions to behavior and find it easier, faster, and clearer in identifying whether or not people did something they were expressly told not to do.

Imagine Moses coming down from Mount Sinai, tablets in hand, only to discover the Israelites partying, whoring, and sacrificing to the golden calf...and being confronted by a team of lawyers out of Egypt suing the organization for human rights violations. What will Moses do? In a traditional organization, Moses will immediately convene a meeting of his board of directors, who will then appoint an investigative task force, who will then review all of the tasks, rules, and procedures Israel was supposed to have followed in the absence of Moses ,while he was on the mountaintop. They will present their defense in court, and together with the legal team for the prosecution they will sift through reports, constitutional bylaws, testimonies, and affidavits. After three years of appeals the court will eventually settle liability. Or, in truth, the litigants will become so tired that they will settle out of court, and true culpability will never be quite clear. The people in Canaan will now lose respect for the integrity of Moses' organization, and prepare to defend Jericho to the death.

On the other hand, Moses might come down from Mount Sinai, tablets in hand, and confront the situation with a servant-empowering mind-set. He will become righteously indignant that specific leaders had clearly done things they were expressly told not to do. He will be able to quickly decide if the prosecutors from Egypt have a legitimate case of human rights violation and settle the dispute quickly and decisively by disciplining the people. The innocent will be affirmed, the victims will be compensated, and the villains will be punished. The credibility of the Israelite organization will soar, and the Canaanites will happily marry their daughters to the sons of Israel.

Clear executive limitations that protect safety and confidentiality are important not only to defend the organization from litigation, but to build trust among the employees and within the mission market. The roots of credibility lie in the confidence people have about fair treatment. When an organization claims a core value, but cannot quickly and decisively adjudicate allegations of sexual harassment in the church choir or denigrating gossip from the church office, the internal morale and external respect plummet. When an organization claims a core value and can quickly determine whether or not the behavior of organizational members delivers that core value, internal morale and external respect soar.

Executive limitations must be carefully considered. They must be aligned to the unique "ends policies" and "process policies" of an organization that is clear about its foundational identity. They must be appropriate to the peculiar context of mission market that is the sphere of influence for the organization's activity. Just as other policies may be shaped for the organization in its entirety and for the major ministries or divisions of that organization, so also the executive limitations can be customized specifically to "block and guide" the behavior of all or some of the volunteers and employees of the organization.

Continuing Education

In the emerging mission market of unpredictable and rapid change, the best way to grow an effective organization is to shape continuing education. The skills you need today will change tomorrow; the team with whom you work so harmoniously today will change next week; the mission market that you addressed so appropriately today changed yesterday. Therefore, everyone must be on a high learning curve. The question is: *What will they be learning?*

The principle of "block and guide" applies to continuing education just as it does to the protection of safety and confidentiality. Servant-empowering organizations use executive limitations to block specific learning methods, learning partnerships, or topics to be able to guide volunteers and staff members toward the learning methods, partners, and topics most appropriate for the *emerging* mission market.

Traditional organizations always pay more attention to acquiring skills than training skills. It is not just a matter of maintaining the comfort zones of volunteers and employees. It is really a matter of control. So long as learning methods, partnerships, and topics remain fundamentally the same, organizational hierarchy can maintain better control over the innovation of employees and minimize the imagination of volunteers. If the organizational members accelerate their learning, then the organizational leaders must accelerate their learning *even faster.* Failure to encourage continuing education is not a means of protecting the comfort zones of the members, but of protecting the comfort zones of the leaders.

The emerging mission market demands that *all continuing education must be outsourced.* It is neither possible, nor desirable, for any organization to develop all of its own training resources and manuals, or teach its newcomers and veterans everything they need to know about the mission market of tomorrow. There are degrees and strategies to outsourcing. Some of the continuing education, especially as related to organizational identity and purpose, must *include* mentors and resources from within the organization. Yet even here, internal training and education must always be partnered with, or supplemented by, teachers and trainers from beyond the organization. The dynamic tension of organizational identity and mission market is preserved and modeled in the very method of training.

In the emerging mission market of unpredictable and rapid change, learning method and partnership have become more important to the design of executive limitations than the topics to be learned.

- Learning methods must be indigenous to the mission market of the organization. If the mission market learns by reading books, the organization trains by reading books. If they learn by listening to lectures, then the organization learns by listening to lectures. However, if the mission market learns through image, video, sound byte, and interactive conversation…the organization must *learn to learn* by image, video, sound byte, and interactive conversation. How you *learn to learn* is just as important to the relevance and effectiveness of organizational mission as what you learn. The question facing organizational leaders is: *How do we need to learn what we need to learn?* Executive limitations will "block" certain options to "guide" people into more indigenous options.
- Learning partnerships must keep pace with the mission market of the organization. The reliability of the "old faithful" academic institutions (business colleges, seminaries, retreat centers, etc.) has now been challenged. Long-distance learning and new information sharing technologies have opened the door to all kinds of formal and informal sources for learning. The tenured faculties and cumbersome bureaucracies of the "academy" and the seniority systems and pervasive biases of parent corporations and denominations impede their ability to partner with individual organizations in their desire to reach the mission market. This does not mean the academy and corporate office are irrelevant. It means that they are no longer *primary*. A plethora of other conversation partners now offer alternatives. The question facing organizational leaders is: *With whom do we need to learn what we need to learn?* It is not a question of downloading information from the right experts, but of partnering with the right people in a common quest to sort out the unknown.
- Learning topics remain important. The problem is that they are always changing. Even the "core curriculums" that were once associated with every organization (accounting for business, social policy for nonprofits, and biblical studies for churches) are changing. Both the interpretation of these topics and the application of these topics are evolving faster and faster. Of course, certain topics will always be core. The problem is that the "core" is always changing. The question facing organizational leaders is: *What is essential to know, at this time, for this mission?* Executive limitations will "block" staff and volunteers from entrenching certain habits, and "guide" them to learn new things.

Traditional organizational leaders try to maintain the effectiveness and relevance of organizational mission through the acquisition of skills and the supervision of actions. Servant-empowering organizational leaders maintain the effectiveness and relevance of organizational mission through continuing education and boundaries within which innovation is free to roam.

For example, a church or nonprofit organization wants to develop a human resources team that will identify, nurture, and train volunteers for the many unpaid leadership roles of the organization. Their core values include servant evangelism; and their bedrock beliefs include the conviction that every human being is gifted and every Christian is called. Their vision is holistic health for individuals and neighborhoods. Their mission is to connect every person with a joyfully fulfilling personal mission that will bless their neighbors.

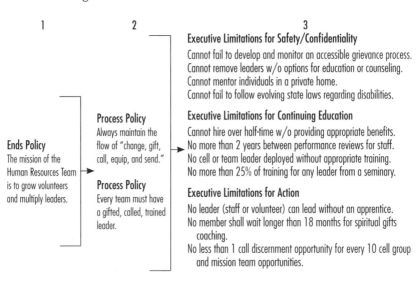

1

2

3

Executive Limitations for Safety/Confidentiality
Cannot fail to develop and monitor an accessible grievance process.
Cannot remove leaders w/o options for education or counseling.
Cannot mentor individuals in a private home.
Cannot fail to follow evolving state laws regarding disabilities.

Process Policy
Always maintain the flow of "change, gift, call, equip, and send."

Executive Limitations for Continuing Education
Cannot hire over half-time w/o providing appropriate benefits.
No more than 2 years between performance reviews for staff.
No cell or team leader deployed without appropriate training.
No more than 25% of training for any leader from a seminary.

Ends Policy
The mission of the Human Resources Team is to grow volunteers and multiply leaders.

Process Policy
Every team must have a gifted, called, trained leader.

Executive Limitations for Action
No leader (staff or volunteer) can lead without an apprentice.
No member shall wait longer than 18 months for spiritual gifts coaching.
No less than 1 call discernment opportunity for every 10 cell group and mission team opportunities.

In this case, the human resources team will be empowered to grow disciples (in accord with whatever guideline of membership is established by the church) and multiply gifted, called, and equipped leaders using any tactic, partner, or resource they wish. However, they must make sure every member is spiritually growing and not stagnating, and they must operate within specific executive limitations. Measurable expectations will help church leaders align the spiritual growth and leadership development habits of the church to their vision and mission.

If this particular example were applied to an emerging social service, health care, or other nonprofit organization, a management team would be empowered to identify, train, and monitor the performance of volunteers from the full demographic and lifestyle diversity of the public. Some of the wording would change, but the principles, processes, and basic executive limitations would free the team from the personal biases of trustees or administrators. They can adapt, initiate, and terminate any program or activity without asking permission, because the board has reasonable trust that the team will be "blocked" and "guided" to align with the overall identity and purpose of the organization.

COORDINATED ACTION

The need to coordinate action in a complex organization is obvious, but the best method to do so is *not* to dictate what everyone can or must do. Increasingly detailed task lists lead to micro-management and stifle creativity. Servant-empowering organizations place the *minimum* restrictions possible to protect the *maximum* freedom for innovation. The organization simply wants to ensure that the creative action of one team does not inhibit the creative action of another team. The rest is up to each team. Two particular issues emerge.

Networking is important, but in the fast-paced world of changing stimuli and unexpected partnerships, it is impossible to dictate from above the dialogue partners for every team. Each team must be empowered to find their own partnerships that are truly effective in getting results. This means that reporting and liaisons must be reduced to a minimum. Few *required* networks or partnerships are imposed on any given team. Reporting and liaisons are not eliminated. They are radically reduced and focused. Team leaders must still interact with other team leaders, for in such forums creativity is stimulated by the creativity of others, and unexpected partnerships are discerned.

Redundancy becomes an ally, not a hindrance. Independent teams pursuing similar goals are not a waste of energy, so long as each team is free to design, implement, and evaluate their progress independently of other teams. This increases the ability of the servant-empowering organization to continuously learn from mistakes. Trial and error, combined with a clear methodology to learn from mistakes and share that learning, is more important than good stewardship of resources. Or, to say it another way, stewardship is not about husbanding program resources. Stewardship is about investing in leadership development. It is wiser for a servant-empowering organization to set several teams loose to discover the absolute best solution to a problem than to limit the quest to one team that will simply develop a mediocre solution to a problem. Better yet, the principle of redundant investment not only discovers multiple solutions, but it grows multiple leaders who will be even better at all problem solving.

For example, a church wants to expand its ministry toward that 42 percent of the public in the three zip codes of their mission field that has no religious affiliation or church background. Their core values include radical hospitality and acceptance; their bedrock beliefs include God's unexplainable healing power and forgiveness. Their vision is to be a waterfall of grace, and their mission is to meet every microculture at the precise point of their personal and spiritual need. Therefore, they align their worship options as follows:

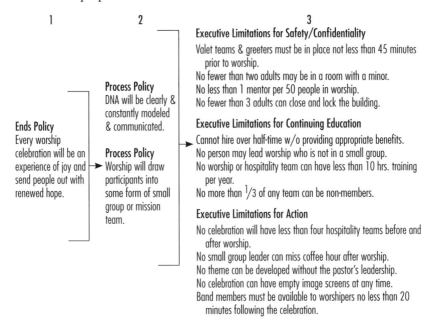

1

2

Process Policy
DNA will be clearly & constantly modeled & communicated.

Ends Policy
Every worship celebration will be an experience of joy and send people out with renewed hope.

Process Policy
Worship will draw participants into some form of small group or mission team.

3

Executive Limitations for Safety/Confidentiality
Valet teams & greeters must be in place not less than 45 minutes prior to worship.
No fewer than two adults may be in a room with a minor.
No less than 1 mentor per 50 people in worship.
No fewer than 3 adults can close and lock the building.

Executive Limitations for Continuing Education
Cannot hire over half-time w/o providing appropriate benefits.
No person may lead worship who is not in a small group.
No worship or hospitality team can have less than 10 hrs. training per year.
No more than 1/3 of any team can be non-members.

Executive Limitations for Action
No celebration will have less than four hospitality teams before and after worship.
No small group leader can miss coffee hour after worship.
No theme can be developed without the pastor's leadership.
No celebration can have empty image screens at any time.
Band members must be available to worshipers no less than 20 minutes following the celebration.

If the worship is boring, fails to motivate a high proportion of participants to attend small groups, or violates any of these executive limitations, church leaders and staff can and must intervene to align congregational identity to mission market. Worship that is *merely* inspirational, or *merely* provides great music, or *merely* delivers sound preaching is not enough, because it does not deliver the outcomes that are expected.

In this particular example, volunteers and staff are empowered to make any reasonable adjustment to worship without getting approvals from a committee. What is "reasonable"? It is an adjustment that clearly makes the goal of worship more relevant and accessible to more microcultures of the mission market–and which more successfully draws newcomers into a 24/7 spiritual formation process. Not only are complaints from church veterans about style, the volume of music, the use of new technologies, or the changed floor plan irrelevant; but the organization empowers worship leaders to say "no" without fear of reprisals from a hierarchy of congregational or denominational management. "Good" worship is "successful" worship, and success is measured by the policies of the organization. It may be that the steepest learning curve to catch up with God in mission is that of the choir director and pastor. So be it. Leaders do not try to slow down the mission market to protect their comfort zones. Leaders accelerate their learning and personal growth to keep up with the mission market.

In an atmosphere of intense spiritual hunger, the only excuse for declining worship attendance is that the policies of the church are hypocritical or the leadership of the church refuses to grow. The policy of the church *says* they want to help all people experience God, but they *behave* in a manner that shapes the worship around the personal needs and tastes of the members. The leaders of the church are called, yet they are unwilling to pay the cost of discipleship by sacrificing personal interest and learning new things.

Note in particular that servant-empowering organizations inevitably offer multiple options in worship. The spiritually yearning public is very diverse and constantly changing. Therefore, the church turns loose multiple teams to address the same challenge. This creative redundancy provides ample opportunity for trial and error, constant learning, and fine tuning. All the teams may be minimally accountable to the pastor or other staff person, but each team is free to partner with any other team that it intuitively feels might contribute to greater success.

A common complaint in the world of declining churches is that "the church should be run like a business." Yet the reality is that this is also a world of *declining businesses!* In fact, the church has always run itself like a business, but it has been even less adaptable to changes in business models than the corporate sector. What *kind* of business model does the church want to imitate? It has already imitated old-fashioned practices of governance by personality, profit, and appeasement; but progressive businesses have already abandoned these models as unsuitable for the chaos and competition of postmodern culture. Policy governance (aimed toward leadership development, team action, and maximum innovation) is the future.

For example, the car rental industry has undergone major revolutions in just the past two decades and is one of the most highly competitive industries today. The old corporate models were rigidly hierarchical, provided few options, burdened employees with endless paperwork, demanded absolute loyalty with few benefits, and were renowned for consumer insensitivity. In other words, they functioned like many churches still function today. All that is changing.

An emerging rental car agency wants to encourage entrepreneurial franchises in a rapidly changing, competitive market and might develop its organizational model as follows. Their core values include honesty, integrity, and respect. Their core convictions are that every human being has hidden potential, and life is more than work. Their vision is mobility with safety. Their mission is to provide the right vehicle, for the right purpose, at the right time.

In this particular example, employees of the rental car agency are free to take initiative within specific boundaries of values and processes. Their goal is to enhance the life of the customer, not just provide transportation. They know that accepting a short-term financial loss in a single service package, offered readily and generously, will encourage a long-term relationship

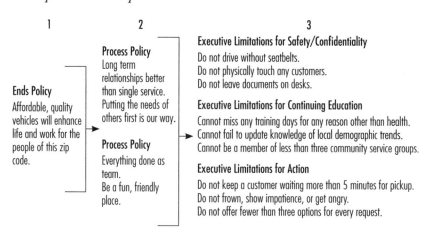

1	2	3
Ends Policy Affordable, quality vehicles will enhance life and work for the people of this zip code.	**Process Policy** Long term relationships better than single service. Putting the needs of others first is our way. **Process Policy** Everything done as team. Be a fun, friendly place.	**Executive Limitations for Safety/Confidentiality** Do not drive without seatbelts. Do not physically touch any customers. Do not leave documents on desks. **Executive Limitations for Continuing Education** Cannot miss any training days for any reason other than health. Cannot fail to update knowledge of local demographic trends. Cannot be a member of less than three community service groups. **Executive Limitations for Action** Do not keep a customer waiting more than 5 minutes for pickup. Do not frown, show impatience, or get angry. Do not offer fewer than three options for every request.

that will eventually translate into higher profits. Yet fundamentally they are not in business to make profit, but to enhance quality of life. This is not just talk. The public is not stupid, and they can sniff hypocrisy when it is in the air. The company trains both an attitude as well as a skill. Good relationships *may* bring more profit; but in this company higher profits *will* be reinvested to grow good relationships and enhance the life of the zip code. The bottom line is that any given employee is empowered to instantly reduce some fee for reasonable cause without ever consulting a manual or asking the boss.

Policy governance is a logical extension of vision discernment under the conditions of the real world. In a perfect world, perhaps, a single brilliant and faithful leader could cast a vision and inspire others to achieve it. The leader would perfectly model core values, perfectly articulate bedrock beliefs, and perfectly understand the mission market. In the real world, all leaders are flawed. Therefore, they must develop an organization to help them approximate perfection.

Conclusion

I described earlier the five necessary steps to make any organization effective and efficient in pursuing the vision. Now we see how each step connects to policy governance.

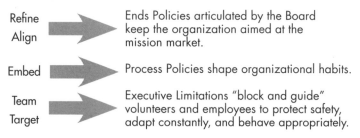

Refine / Align → Ends Policies articulated by the Board keep the organization aimed at the mission market.

Embed → Process Policies shape organizational habits.

Team / Target → Executive Limitations "block and guide" volunteers and employees to protect safety, adapt constantly, and behave appropriately.

Not only do we see how the steps for effective and efficient visioning connect with policy governance, but we also begin to understand the roles of organizational leaders. In a perfect world, a single pastor or CEO might have the authenticity, integrity, sensitivity, and skillfulness to aim everyone, train everyone, and monitor everyone to fulfill the vision. In the real world the pastor or CEO needs help.

- The board of directors will help refine and align policy.
- Any and all leaders, of any group, large or small, will embed policy.
- The management team will help team and target policy.

If leaders do this, the volunteers and staff employees are empowered to do the work. Leaders do not do the work. They refine, align, embed, target, and team the policy. The people do the work, and they are empowered to be as aggressively innovative as possible in carrying out the work. They do not need permission to do work. They simply must live within specific boundaries and avoid doing certain things.

Now we understand why traditional organizations and organizational leaders (in business, nonprofit, church, government, and every sector) resist policy governance and are uncomfortable with a truly servant-empowering organization.

- *The cult of personality and patronage is shattered.* Suddenly leaders must let go of control and are forced to trust. While they may complain about their burdensome workloads, they secretly enjoy the prestige and power. Suddenly volunteers and employees are given control and forced to grow. Leaders don't want to let go of control and hesitate to trust. Members don't want the responsibility of leadership and don't want to grow. They secretly want somebody else to take the blame so they can go home to supper. The servant-empowering organization forces the boss to get a life and forces the employees to get down to work.
- *Profit becomes a means to a greater good.* However you measure institutional success (by financial profit, membership increase, program development, or market share), institutional success no longer is the real goal. Community life is the real goal. The institution is important as a means to an end and ceases to become an end in itself. The members are empowered and the mission market is reached, but along the way the entire institution is continually reinventing itself. What is sacred is effective mission, not institutional survival.
- *Outcomes for personal and social change become primary.* The internal harmony, comfort, or peacefulness of the organization is continually *risked* for the sake of positive outcomes beyond the organization. Urgency replaces serenity in the workplace. This does not mean that quality relationships and good friendships are irrelevant in the organization,

but that they are not the goal of the organization. The members are not the mission. The strangers are the mission; the zip code is the mission. Volunteers and staff are pushed to the edge of anticipation, motivated for constant learning, ready to make personal adjustments to more effectively accomplish the mission.

Policy governance removes personality, profit, and appeasement from center stage in the life and work of any organization. It allows for changing personnel; it sustains organizational purpose through fluctuations in finance and membership; and it protects the organization from the emotional blackmail of special interests. Most importantly, however, policy governance preserves the passion and purpose of mission.

The Basic Structure

Servant-empowering organizations must be *experienced* to be *understood*. This is in marked contrast to traditional organizations, which must be *understood* to be *experienced*. The servant-empowering organization emerges from the constant challenge for market relevance and mission alignment in the fast-paced world of change. It is fluid before it is solid; it is intuitive before it is rational; it is a movement before it is an institution. The art of leadership in the servant-empowering organization is always to introduce barely controlled chaos into the organizational structure. The moment the organization becomes *fully* understandable and solidifies to become a rational institution, it loses momentum. Both relevance and alignment begin to waver.

The Early Church's Changing Structure

Ironically, the earliest church modeled the servant-empowering organization. No one would describe St. Paul and the early apostles as "management theorists," but their choice of the living organism as the basic metaphor of the church led inexorably to the dynamic of consensus and team. See next page for a snapshot of their policy governance strategy.

This chain of policymaking linked the organizational identity of the earliest church with their mission to multiply disciples of Jesus Christ. Failure to live within these boundaries elicited intervention from St. Paul and rebuke from the author of Revelation. Credible leadership modeled and taught these policies. It is safer to say that apostolic succession had less to do with office holding, personal charisma, or success, but rather had everything to do with preserving and passing on this chain of policies to the next generation.

The organizational shift from office-based to team-based mission is the undercurrent of stress in the first 15 chapters of the Acts of the Apostles. The church responded to the chaos and competition in the mission market of the first and second centuries by radically decentralizing its organizational structure and investing in leadership development and the deployment of highly trusted teams. The New Testament really only tracks one such

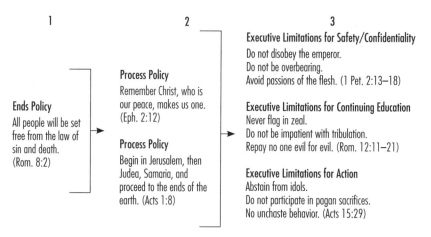

1

Ends Policy
All people will be set free from the law of sin and death. (Rom. 8:2)

2

Process Policy
Remember Christ, who is our peace, makes us one. (Eph. 2:12)

Process Policy
Begin in Jerusalem, then Judea, Samaria, and proceed to the ends of the earth. (Acts 1:8)

3

Executive Limitations for Safety/Confidentiality
Do not disobey the emperor.
Do not be overbearing.
Avoid passions of the flesh. (1 Pet. 2:13–18)

Executive Limitations for Continuing Education
Never flag in zeal.
Do not be impatient with tribulation.
Repay no one evil for evil. (Rom. 12:11–21)

Executive Limitations for Action
Abstain from idols.
Do not participate in pagan sacrifices.
No unchaste behavior. (Acts 15:29)

team, alludes to several others, and does not even describe teams led by other apostles that we know impacted other cultures and nations. Yet it is clear that these teams had real power to discern, design, implement, and evaluate mission without having to seek approvals from the head office in Jerusalem—provided, of course, that they stayed within certain boundaries that were the consensus of the church.

This organizational model is one major reason why the earliest church was able to spread its faith so rapidly across the Roman world, and why the Roman world was powerless to stop it. The Roman world remained office-based and highly centralized. It simply did not know how to address a movement that was so team-based and highly decentralized. It was only after the Christian movement became "official" and was codified to imitate Roman administration that it began to fragment, turn in upon itself, and stop growing. Every reformation of the church has introduced barely controlled (and sometimes quite uncontrolled) chaos to take the church beyond the institutional, and back to the experiential.

Organizational change is always precipitated by systemic upheaval; but organizational change by itself rarely *precipitates* systemic change. The principle can be applied not only to religious organizations, but to every organization—including political governments, corporate businesses, and social services. The organization emerges as a movement and must be experienced to be understood; then it solidifies into an institution that must be understood to be controlled. To remain market relevant and missionally aligned, it must be returned to its fluid state once again. This is the art of political, corporate, or nonprofit leadership.

Servant-empowering Structure

Unfortunately, to *explain* the structure of the servant-empowering organization I must resort to words. The linear requirements of grammar and syntax automatically force the structure to be cast in a rational, solidified, institutional way. Subsequent chapters will try to restore the dynamic quality of the organizational model.

The basic organizational structure looks like this:[1]

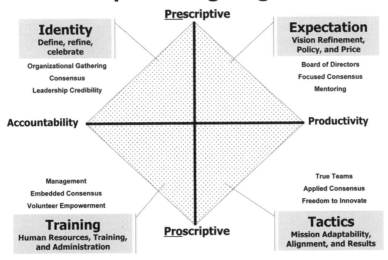

The Empowering Organization

- The quadrants above the horizontal line are "*pre*scriptive," in the sense that all aspects of the organization must align with a clear vision and mission and must live within specific boundaries of core values and beliefs, ends policies, and procedural habits. The quadrants below the horizontal line are "*pro*scriptive," in the sense that organizational leaders and teams are "blocked" from specific actions in order to be "guided" for safety, continuous learning, and coordination.
- The quadrants to the left of the vertical line are all about "accountability," in the sense that core values and beliefs are transparent to every member of the organization, and management builds reasonable trust by embedding habits and monitoring limitations. The quadrants to the right of the vertical line are all about "productivity," in the sense that boards measure results with ends policies, and teams are empowered to be innovative and creative to achieve results.

---

[1] I am indebted to the many books by John and Miriam Mayhew Carver, and strongly recommend reading *Boards That Make a Difference* (San Francisco: Jossey-Bass, 1990) and *Reinventing Your Board* (San Francisco: Jossey-Bass, 1997). Terminology and key ideas such as "prescriptive," "proscriptive," and "policy governance" reveal my debt, but the particular interpretations and applications to the church and organic organizational life are, for better or worse, entirely my own.

The servant-empowering organization has four key pieces. Each piece has a sphere of influence defined by its function in the diagram.[2]

Identity

The identity of the organization is its foundation of trust. This is the general consensus of values, beliefs, vision, and mission that lies at the heart of the movement. Traditional organizations become so obsessed with structure and control that they lose clarity about this identity. This is called "institutionalization," or the rational abstraction of what began as a missional movement. Recovery of the vitality of this identity is crucial.

Identity is what feeds the credibility of leadership and drives any organizational gathering. The more leadership becomes limited to expertise, and the more gatherings are relegated to management, the more the organization loses relevance and alignment. Organizational identity is *prescriptive* in that it defines, refines, and celebrates what *must be true* in every aspect of the life of the organization. It is the primary vehicle of accountability.

Therefore, every gathering of the entire organization, whether for recreation or information, is a "culture-shaping" event. It refines the identity or spirit of the organization that will be embodied in the leaders and transparent to the public through even the lowliest employee or smallest program. Every gathering, even the corporate Christmas party, is part of the accountability and prescriptive lifestyle of the organization.

Expectation

Expectations for any organization are refined and focused by a core of credible leaders at the heart of the organization. They are "representative" only in the sense that they "represent" or "visibly reveal" in their own work and lifestyles the identity that is the consensus of the organization. They are not "representative" in the sense that they are elected by, or are accountable to, any particular faction or administrative unit of the organization. The spirit of the organization is most clearly modeled in the behavior and planning of the leaders.

Expectations are refined both by defining anticipated results and by focusing the price to be paid to achieve those results. This is not a management role, but a policy and leadership development function. Organizational expectations are *prescriptive* in the sense that they identify what *must result* if the organization is effectively pursuing its mission. It is the primary vehicle for measuring productivity or success.

Therefore, every board meeting is a "mission-aligning" event. The board refines the vision and connects it to the mission field, making the big decisions that will guide the strategic path of the organization. Every

---

[2]This chart is based on an original found in my book *Christian Chaos* (Nashville: Abingdon Press, 1995).

board meeting shapes the prescriptive lifestyle of management and teams, and contributes to the productivity of the organization.

Training

Rigorous and constant training for employees or volunteers is the key to success. The servant-empowering organization must have a trusted, gifted few who coordinate the ongoing work and equip leaders to innovate their way to mission results. Training is more than skills development. It is leadership development. It is all about growing people with the attitude, integrity, ability, and teamwork that will accomplish the vision and mission that is the consensus of the organization.

Training includes everything from discerning gifts and calls, questing for quality, protecting safety and confidentiality, and managing resources and calendars. Fundamentally, however, management is not about *controlling* but about *equipping*. It is *pro*scriptive because the most effective training does not limit continuous learning to specific tasks, but prohibits continuing education from becoming entrenched. It is the second vehicle of accountability.

Therefore, staff deployment and management meetings are "leader-developing" events. What is "administrated" is not program development but personal growth. Management is even willing to accept strategic mediocrity, if in so doing a mentoring moment is created that will take organizational members to a higher level of performance. Every interaction and conversation between management and team is part of accountability to mission, and empowerment for innovation.

Tactics

"Tactics" encompasses all of the activity that discerns, designs, implements, and evaluates mission initiatives. In the servant-empowering organization, this is accomplished through entrepreneurial partnerships called "true teams." These teams apply the identity of the organization to mission marketplace.

True teams are free to be absolutely creative within the constraints of the consensus of identity that the core leaders of the organization have refined and focused. Therefore, true teams function *pro*scriptively by simply avoiding things that the organization expressly forbids. They are also the sharp edge of productivity that finally accomplishes the anticipated results of the organization.

Therefore, team action (including programs, partnerships, fund-raising, and everything else related to the pragmatic implementation of mission) is always a "mission-achieving" event. Teams are free to do whatever it takes, within certain boundaries, to achieve the overall mission of the organization. The team is the primary mission unit of the organization, operating within specific executive limitations, for maximum productivity.

Conclusion

I have deliberately avoided imposing any particular assumptions about the internal nature of these four pieces of the servant-empowering organization. These are best explained in the context of the organizational *dynamics.* In the end, the servant-empowering organization cannot be fully contained, explained, or understood by grammar and syntax. In the same way, traditional organizational by-laws and rules will be unable to interpret it, and, if thoroughly imposed, will only institutionalize a movement and precipitate increasing irrelevance and misalignment. This is an organization *without by-laws.* It is an organization that is fluid, highly adaptable, and driven by results.

Ultimately, the servant-empowering organization is not about program management. This is the focus of traditional institutions. As a fluid *movement,* the servant-empowering organization is really about *leadership development.* It concentrates on growing employees and volunteers to passionately and automatically live within a specific consensus and strive to achieve specific mission results. The goal is not to maintain programs but to deploy entrepreneurial leaders who can own the mission themselves.

The Dynamic of Consensus and Team

The Nature of Consensus

The Basic Unit of Mission

The Dynamic of Consensus
and Team

A "dynamic" is a fluid movement in the life of an organization that is constantly repeated, yet subtly different every time. It is predictable in its occurrence, but unpredictable in its result. A "dynamic" is like the movement of waves breaking on the seashore. The waves are repetitive, yet each time they break on the shore with differences in intensity, direction, and impact. These differences may be subtle or dramatic, depending on the conditions of wind, sun, sand, and the changing environment.

The dynamic of consensus and team is the first of three fundamental dynamics at the heart of a servant-empowering organization. Remember, consensus is not about abstractions and agreements, but about shared core values, bedrock beliefs, motivating vision, and strategic mission. Consensus creates, impels, and guides each team as it impacts the mission market. Yet each team will adapt to the environment, and impact the mission market, in unpredictable intensity and direction. On this side, teams will create a new "sand dune," and on that side teams will undermine an old institution and create a new inlet. Consensus is the driving force and true teams are the visible agents of mission that sculpt, and re-sculpt, the cultural landscape.

Potency of Consensus

The nature of consensus will be explored in the next chapter, but it is important to understand that consensus is the potency of organizational life. It is latent energy, not simply a static collection of ideals, dogmas, and dreams. Consensus is the volatile confluence of forces that generates passion. This is because "consensus" is the foundation of trust. It is the depth of being in organizational life, and out of the depths emerge the waves of outreach that will impact the world. The deeper the consensus is, the more powerful the waves become. If the consensus is shallow, the waves may create a roiling surface that is all show but little force. If the consensus is deep, the waves will create huge rollers that crash against the seashore and transform the mission market.

Trust as the Depth of Consensus

Trust is that depth. Create a profound environment of trust, and people will become leaders, and leaders will become innovators, and innovators will gather disciples, and together they will change the world. But you must trust them first! They must be convinced they are trusted. You must be able to release them…turn them loose…unshackle them from control…and allow them to impact the mission market in unpredictable ways.

Trust is also the confidence that once the true team has impacted the mission market, it will then "recede" back into the depths of consensus to regroup, refocus, and regain momentum for another initiative, and another initiative, and another initiative, *ad infinitum.* The energy of the team will not be left on the beach, so to speak, where it will evaporate in the sun or be trapped in stagnant pools. It must recede back into the depths of consensus to be reenergized.

What happens to employees and volunteers when they realize they are actually trusted is remarkable. They come alive. Traditional organizations treat employees and volunteers like zombies ("the walking dead"). Zombies are easy to control. Command them to go or come; sit in meetings or sell products; and they will do it. They will unswervingly do what they are told to do. Yet they will be dead inside. Their very lack of imagination, and their powerlessness to take risks, ultimately kills the company. This is because the creativity of the organization is limited by the imagination or faithfulness of the boss, or a handful of empowered people.

Need for Freedom

A traditional organization only grows to the size of the controller with the least imagination. Six other bosses with great competence will all be limited by the least-imaginative seventh controller. The company can fire or replace that controller, of course, but that does not solve the intrinsic problem. The problem is that most of the employees and volunteers are walking dead people. Redundant levels of management are supervising them constantly, because at the deepest level of consciousness the company believes its employees will instinctively and naturally do something illegal, immoral, or irresponsibly expensive if they don't control them. The employees and volunteers know it. Their eyes glaze over; their motions become stilted; they do what they are told and no more; they protect their privileges and no more; they watch the clock, complain if they are held back, and can't wait to be free. It is a classic definition of a zombie…and of most established church members. But what if they were free?

The great mistake in most churches (and other organizations) is the assumption that *love* leads to *freedom.* Churches go out of their way to express *love* for the members, expecting this will motivate more volunteerism, higher stewardship, and greater participation. This love is demonstrated by knowing their first names, celebrating a member's birthday, and offering constant care-giving through all the stages of life. Translated to other sectors, this means companies go out of their way to *appreciate* their employees and volunteers with parties, perks, and bonuses. It doesn't work. Being *loved* never motivates *service*. It never improves *productivity*. In fact, it encourages even greater passivity. It does not free them to serve, but tempts them to be served all the more. It makes the life of the zombie not only bearable, but a pretty good deal if you can get it.

Trust leads to *freedom!* The resurrection of Christ led to the great commissioning. Not until the disciples were *trusted* with a mission did they truly become *alive*. Trust does that to people. The greater the trust, the more they sacrifice. The deeper the trust, the more they are free to take risks for the sake of the mission. The same is true in any organization. When employees and volunteers are convinced that they are not only loved, but actually *trusted* to carry on mission, the more they come alive. They no longer walk with glazed eyes, but begin to observe and interact with their environment with open eyes. They begin to innovate and take pride in corporate success.

Teams as the Organization's Action Unit

Teams are the primary mission action unit of the organization. Committees and task groups are the instruments to manage zombies. True teams are the instruments to focus and turn loose leaders who are *alive*. The primary reference point for every team is the consensus of the organization, rather than the central administration of the organization. In other words, they receive permission to initiate work from their own ability to discern and interpret the consensus of the organization. They do not require permission from an intermediate bureaucracy that interprets the consensus for them. They use the consensus of the organization–the "spirituality" of the organization–as the context from which mission and imagination emerge, and they are free to follow that mission. They do not need to rely on a hierarchy to tell them what to do. This is the fundamental dynamic of high trust typical of servant-empowering organizations.

At the same time, each team must be held rigorously accountable to operate within boundaries that are the consensus of the organization. The "wave" has freedom to break upon the shoreline, but it must recede into the depths of the ocean once again. The team has freedom to discern, design, implement, and evaluate mission; but the evaluation means that to renew its strength the team must return to the core values, beliefs, vision, and mission that is the depth of the organization.

Conclusion

The adapted chart below tries to capture the dynamic of consensus and team. The shared identity of values, beliefs, vision, and mission that lies at the depth of organizational life elicits the action of true teams. It is an environment of trust, and trust makes people come alive. True teams emerge like waves, repetitively impacting the mission market to sculpt the cultural landscape. They are free to focus, adapt, and change in any way they wish to accomplish mission results, but only within specific boundaries of integrity defined by the depths of organizational life. They then "recede" into that depth of identity to evaluate success and ensure alignment with the vision of the organization.

The movement of the wave is repetitive: from accountability to productivity and from productivity to accountability. For every act of accountability, there is an exponential act of productivity; and for every exponential act of productivity, there is an inevitable act of accountability. What is most visible at the top of the wave, and in the activity of the true team, is the identity of the organization. This is shaped by the expectations of the core leadership or visionary board. This is "prescriptive" because it is the positive expression of what the organization wants to be and do. What is least visible, but of equal importance, is the training of the team. This is shaped by core equippers or management of the organization. This is "proscriptive" because it is the limitation defining what teams *cannot* be and do.

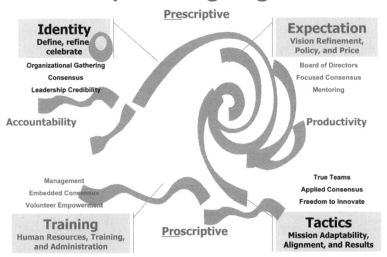

The Empowering Organization

The dynamic of consensus and team is what makes the waves dance and the organization come alive. Board and management play important functions, and represent a second dynamic in organizational life. They are not what is most visible in organizational life. To experience a servant-empowering organization is to experience, first and foremost, the dynamic of consensus and teams. This is what attracts newcomers to the church and the best, brightest talents to the company. In traditional organizations, it is board and management that are most visible in organizational life. They hope that the charisma of the CEO or the personnel benefits of the organization will attract new people. Yet the public is no longer willing to be dead to make a living. They want to both make a living and be fully *alive*.

The Nature of Consensus

Consensus is crucial to organizational life, because without it the organization possesses no foundation for trust. Consensus is particularly crucial to servant-empowering organizational life, because reasonable trust is the very stuff of which true teams are made. Innovation and creativity are only possible in an environment of trust, and trust is only possible in the context of a clear consensus about the spirituality of the organization.

Defining Consensus

The Enlightenment Definition

Yet "consensus" is one of the most misunderstood and misapplied concepts in modernity. This is because the Enlightenment, and its by-products of mechanism and scientism, assumed that the universe was made of independent units in external relationship to each other. The only way to *understand* life was to analyze it from the unity of greatest generality to the diversity of greatest specificity: from species, to genus, to agent. The only way to *organize* people was to structure them in a hierarchy of authority. Since things and people were absolutely individual, and only externally related to each other, the only way to achieve results was to impose redundant levels of oversight to make sure every potentially rogue individual was performing assigned tasks for the greater good. In the world, this "great chain of redundant oversight" began with God, descended to angels, then to bishops and official church leaders, then to committee chairpersons, and so on. In organizational life, this oversight began with the CEO, descended to the board, then to supervisors and middle managers, and finally to the average laborer with a long task list. In essence, the laborers literally had multiple supervisors looking over their shoulders every morning when they stamped their time cards.

Modernity replaced "consensus" with redundant oversight–and then renamed redundant oversight as "consensus." Reasonable trust was not only unnecessary, but potentially dangerous. After all, life itself was only made up of independent units externally related to each other. Life was a billiard table on which rogue balls needed to be racked in a triangle so that omnipotent God could break. Organizational life, therefore, was only made up of independent individuals externally related to each other. Organizations were a gaggle of unruly individuals requiring a higher authority to send them where they needed to go.

A Postmodern Intuition

What if the Enlightenment, and its by-products, were wrong? What if the universe is not made up of independent units in external relationship to each other, but mutually dependent units in internal relationship to each other? This is not the place to explore the revolution in metaphysics that has begun to recognize that the internal constitution of everything in life is intrinsically tied to the intrinsic constitution of everything else in life. That intuition, however, has also revolutionized perceptions of organizational life. Organizations founded on the conviction that its members are fundamentally *untrustworthy* cannot survive long. Organizations founded on the conviction that their members fundamentally share certain purposes, motivations, behavioral expectations, and convictions thrive. This intrinsic trust cannot be imposed from a hierarchy. It must be nurtured in, and arise from, the hearts of the employees and volunteers.

Consensus as Three Kinds of Unanimity

Consensus comes in three kinds of unanimity. Together these provide a "united amity" in the life of an organization. This is a unity of mutual respect, interrelated support, and shared joy that makes the organization predisposed to function well. Cooperation is a behavioral *habit*. Integrity is an automatic *assumption*. Purposefulness is a performance *routine*.

Unanimity of Spirit

Servant-empowering organizations have a clear consensus about the "spirituality" of the organization. They have fundamental reasons to trust one another because each member of the organization shares specific core values, bedrock beliefs, motivating vision, and strategic mission.

These are embedded in the hearts and minds of employees and volunteers to such an extent that patterns of behavior that are visibly unique to the organization are automatic. There is an *espirit de corps* at the heart of the organization so that even the lowliest part-timer can say with pride, *"We are* this *company rather than* that *company."*

Unanimity of Confidence

Servant-empowering organizations have a wholehearted confidence in leadership. They are convinced that the leaders who refine the point of mission, shape policy, and determine the price of success are *credible spiritual leaders*. That is to say, they model the "spirit" of the organization, are driven by the "spirit" of the organization, and are capable of aligning the organization to live in that "spirit" without sidetracks or temptations.

The organization and each of its members are ready to follow leaders even into danger or sacrifice because the leaders embody the very purpose of organizational life.

Unanimity of Assent

Servant-empowering organizations expect absolute commitment to ideas, strategies, and tactics *within the team.* Unanimity of assent is not required for the overall ideas, strategies, and tactics of the organization; but it is essential within each team. Team members must all agree that the particular actions they develop, initiate, and evaluate are clearly aligned with the "spirit" of the organization and the policies of credible leaders. There is no "minority vote" in the function of a true team. The true team only acts when every member of the team is absolutely committed.

United Amity in Contrast with Consensus Management

This "united amity" of the servant-empowering organization is a stark contrast to the so-called "consensus management" of traditional (post-Enlightenment) organizations. Traditional organizations demand assent for every tactic, strategy, and budget line. Either every member of the organization must *obey* the task-driven agendas of the hierarchy, or every member of the organization must *vote* on the task-driven agendas of the organization. In this light, no real difference exists between "Episcopal" and "Presbyterian" governance. Their supposed differences are really a post-Enlightenment quibble between organizational cousins. Similarly, no real difference separates "monarchies" and "democracies." The basic premise of each is that, one way or another, every member of the organization must *assent* to every tactic or strategy proposed. In the time it takes for authoritarian hierarchies to gain the obedience of their employees, or for representative democracies to gain agreement from all their employees, the world has moved on, and the opportunity has been lost.

The "united amity" of the servant-empowering organization avoids the necessity of assent by the entire organization about every tactic, because it establishes reasonable trust. There is unanimous participation in the "spirit" of the organization and unanimous confidence in the leadership of the organization. However, the functioning of the servant-empowering organization demands *absolute assent in the context of every single team.* Teams must be able to act as a single mind. The true team necessarily becomes the primary working unit of the organization. More than any office, staff person, or individual, the true team is the primary "agent" of the mission.

Layers of Consensus

From the point of view of the true team, "layers" of consensus mark the life of the servant-empowering organization. These correspond to the elements of policy governance described in the previous chapter.

- *Consensus:* This is the unanimity of spirit and unanimity of confidence in leadership that is the "united amity" of the organization. These are the broadest boundaries beyond which no team can go. These are the behavior patterns and purposes embedded in the heart of every team.
- *Focused Consensus:* These are the "ends policies" developed by the credible leaders in whom the organization has extraordinary confidence. These policies refine the point of mission and define the anticipated, measurable results in personal and social change. Leaders define for every team the degree of sacrifice, or the price of success, that any team must be prepared to pay for the sake of the mission.
- *Habitual Consensus:* These are the "process policies" or working habits crucial to efficient management and leadership development of the organization. These are minimal, and may change as the cultural context evolves. Yet at any given time they are the norms of behavior with which every team synchronizes itself with every other team.
- *Applied Consensus:* These are the "executive limitations" uniquely developed within each team, relevant to the context and content of their work, which protect safety, guide learning, and facilitate networking with other agencies. These may also change over time, but they are the proscriptive boundaries that define actions explicitly denied.

All these represent layers of consensus in the servant-empowering organization. Within this consensus, true teams are trusted to discern, design, implement, and evaluate mission in any way they wish.

The layers of consensus correspond to the four quadrants in the diagram for the servant-empowering organization. Each piece of the organization reveals the "united amity" of the organization in a distinct way.

Consensus *itself is revealed through large organizational gatherings of any kind.*

In a nonprofit organization, this could be anything from an annual meeting to a corporate picnic. In a church, it may be a congregational gathering or a worship service. The only organizational function of such gatherings is that they define, refine, and celebrate the "spirituality" (core values, beliefs, vision, and mission) of the organization. Such gatherings do not approve or disapprove of anything. They are not management meetings. They do not review budgets, approve tactics, or listen to reports. To do so would be an obvious sign of lack of confidence in leaders.

Instead, these gatherings focus entirely on communicating, focusing, and embedding the values, beliefs, vision, and mission that is the heart of the organization. Employees and staff see the "spirituality" of the organization in the behavior of their leaders, the behavior of the members, and the posture of the organization as a whole. This embeds the "spirituality" of the organization in the hearts of the teams, so that they automatically discern the most fundamental boundaries for their actions.

Focused Consensus is revealed through the activities of the board.

One of the functions of a visionary board is to focus the "spirituality" of the organization on the mission market in all of its diversity. It does not redefine, but *refines,* consensus. It does this partly by establishing "ends policies," but also by modeling in its behavior the very identity of the organization, and then by mentoring new organizational members to embed that same identity. From the point of view of true teams, board members function as mentors and examples to the team leaders.

Habitual Consensus is revealed through the activities of leaders at all levels.

Leaders in every context (board, management, or teams) will set minimal, but crucial procedural policies for the organizational members in their sphere of influence. These "procedures," however, are not requirements for purposes of reporting, but normative approaches to problem solving. They are really "habits." They are often automatic, but quite intentional methods with which organizational members address a challenge, resolve a problem, or pursue mission, which are consistent with the "spirituality" of the organization. From the point of view of true teams, habitual consensus is the methodology that is logically implied by shared values, beliefs, vision, and mission.

Applied Consensus is revealed through true teams.

True teams are the primary unit of work in a servant-empowering organization. They take the consensus of the organization (focused and embedded into the behavior of the staff and volunteers), and innovate ways to apply it to the diversity of the mission market. This interface is the chaos of culture. The rapidly changing mission market fragments and recombines in unique ways. Teams must scramble to remain relevant to the mission market (human need) and aligned to deliver the mission product (experience of blessing). To do that, they simplify accountability by abandoning task lists and adopting executive limitations.

Conclusion

Consensus is profoundly different in the servant-empowering organization from traditional organizations. The four layers of consensus do *not* represent layers of authority. This is not a chain of reporting, adjudicating, and permission-giving in a hierarchy of management. Consensus does not consist in agreement about tactics. Instead, the layers of consensus represent spheres of influence. Each sphere has complete freedom to make decisions and initiate action without reporting or obtaining permission from another sphere, but within the accountability of shared values, beliefs, vision, and mission.

We need to re-visualize the original diagram of one diamond with four quadrants, and imagine a more dynamic diagram like this:

The Empowering Organization

Each piece of the organizational model has its own sphere of influence. Each piece intersects with the others at crucial points to focus consensus, embed habits of consensus, and apply consensus. The dotted line represents the general consensus or "spirituality" of the organization beyond which innovation cannot go. The diagram only identifies a single team. Imagine the multiplication of *multitudes* of teams spinning around the gravitational pull of organizational "spirituality" and reaching out in creative ways.

The Basic Unit of Mission

In a servant-empowering organization, the basic unit of work is a true team. Literally everything, from the most complex program or ministry to the simplest secretarial or custodial task, is accomplished as a team. A "team" is not another word for "task group" or "committee." True teams have real power to discern, design, implement, and evaluate mission without having to appeal to an outside authority. Task groups and committees never have such power and are constantly writing reports, seeking approvals, and waiting for permission. True teams can only exist in a context of high trust. They function most effectively in a context of policy governance.

Characteristics of a Team

If the fundamental dynamic of consensus and team can be envisioned as a "wave" of water, the true team is best compared to a water droplet. How large is a "droplet"? It may be as small as a single molecule or as large as a sheet of water. Teams are not defined by any particular size, but by three characteristics of fluids:

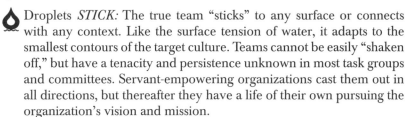 Droplets *STICK:* The true team "sticks" to any surface or connects with any context. Like the surface tension of water, it adapts to the smallest contours of the target culture. Teams cannot be easily "shaken off," but have a tenacity and persistence unknown in most task groups and committees. Servant-empowering organizations cast them out in all directions, but thereafter they have a life of their own pursuing the organization's vision and mission.

Droplets *DRIP:* The true team moves along the surface or follows the contours of any context. They are opportunistic, following the lines of least resistance, and eventually undermining and overcoming any obstacle until the target is saturated by the core values and bedrock beliefs of the organization. True teams change or "travel" with a freedom and spontaneity unknown in most task groups and committees. Their progress is not controlled by an authority beyond the team, but is influenced by the emerging changes (opportunities and obstacles) of the mission field.

Droplets *MERGE:* True teams readily merge with another, or separate from one another, as the conditions of the mission market require. No artificial barriers are formed by office or mandate. Teams face no one internally or externally with a need to defend a sphere of authority. The teams can readily grow larger or smaller to become more effective. Unlike task groups or committees, true teams can reshape or restructure themselves instantly and immediately. They are radically pragmatic and results driven.

The peculiarly fluid nature of the true team to "stick, drip, and merge" makes them potent entrepreneurial partnerships. Yet this is only possible because the "molecular structure" of each droplet is identical. They all share the same values, beliefs, vision, and mission. They all enjoy high trust.

A Team's Structure and Interaction

The way a team is structured and the way team members interact vary considerably according to the mission of the organization. Lack of clarity about the mission of the organization will result in the multiplication of inappropriate or ineffective teams. Much of the organizational literature today uses the organic terminology of "cells," which I have found useful in theory but impractical for coaching. However, if we think of a team as a cell, then the multiplication of inappropriately or ineffectively designed teams resulting from lack of mission clarity can be compared to a "cancer" in the organism. These are teams that structure themselves and that interact within and beyond themselves in ways that may be entirely appropriate in one kind of mission-driven organization, but which are quite inappropriate in another organization.

Do not allow yourself to be caught up in metaphors. Teams have been explained in the language of professional sports, amateur sports, improvisational jazz, symphony orchestras, chat rooms, exploration expeditions, military companies, ship crews, insect colonies, botanical species, research laboratories, and extended families. All these metaphors can make sense for particular kinds of organizations, but not for others.

- One can easily imagine a team *functioning like* a jazz ensemble, with no verbal commands and only eye contact, no predictable routines but only gut intuition, for an organization with a missional purpose for mysticism. One cannot, however, apply such a metaphor to a team in an engineering company with a missional purpose to design safe suspension bridges. Teams are not really about processes, but results that bring lasting positive change.
- One can easily imagine a team *functioning like* a sports team with a strong perfectionism about performance and a strong goal to win. This makes sense of some organizations driven by obtaining contracts or meeting quotas, but they do not make sense for organizations with a mission to

acquaint seekers with Christ. The pastor or team leader cannot easily be cast in the role of "quarterback," and mission success cannot easily be measured as "scoring points." Teams are really not about "winning," but about trial and error, persistence, and shaping culture.

When you allow the definition of a team to become entangled with a particular metaphor, you run the risk of multiplying teams designed for the wrong missional purpose. *Missional purpose dictates the unique design of the team.*

This is why I have used the metaphor of "the wave" and the power of waves to cast "droplets" on the "shoreline" of the mission market. It is these droplets that shape the marketplace by their ability to "stick, drip, and merge." The power of teams does not lie in a single team, but in the succession of teams beating against the shoreline, or the plethora of teams adapting to every nuance of cultural diversity. Teams have an origin in the depths of organizational life, and a relentless purposefulness as they pursue the mission of organizational life. Servant-empowering organizations, like waves, send out a "spray" of teams that impact the mission market.

True Team Leadership

The multiplication of true teams depends entirely on the rigorous pursuit of leadership development. Traditional organizations pretend that their task groups and committees are teams, but in fact they resist true teams. The most common response from traditional organizational leaders is this:

I can get the job done better and faster if I just do it myself!

They regard the time invested to grow and train teams as a waste of energy, believing that it will take too long and never achieve the quality result that will allow the organization to remain productive and stay ahead of the competition. The paradox is that traditional organizations become so obsessed by productivity that they become less productive. They become so worried about remaining competitive that they become less relevant. For a short time one or more key organizational leaders may indeed have such competence and creativity that by personal efforts alone they can keep the organization growing. Yet they burn out, drop out, or opt out. Then the traditional organization cannot replace them. Inevitably, the more traditional organizations rely upon a few people being extraordinarily productive, the more quickly these organizations become less productive.

Although examples of this paradox abound in all sectors, no illustration is clearer than that of the local church. Clergy, staff, and a handful of capable volunteers constantly ignore leadership development to be more productive. The most common complaint is that 20 percent of the people do all of the work, while 80 percent of the people watch and enjoy the benefits. The more demands pile up on the clergy and staff, the harder they work, the less time they invest in developing other leaders, the more readily they burn out, and the less productive the mission becomes.

Dysfunctional Assumptions in Traditional Organizations

This paradox about productivity reveals deeper dysfunctional assumptions at the heart of traditional organizations and traditional organizational leaders. Behind the conviction, "The job could be done better and faster if I just did it myself," lie these hidden convictions:

- If I do it myself, I will get all the praise and glory;
- If I do it myself, I will be able to control the organization;
- If I do it myself, I can contain productivity within the boundaries of my own comfort zones.

The hidden dysfunction of non-team-based organizations is that *no one can really and truly* be trusted *other than oneself.* This is why traditional organizations resist the concept of true teams. The potential of true teams challenges the arrogance of North American leaders.

Growing More Leaders

Every true team must have a leader whose primary responsibility is to grow and equip more leaders. Productivity is secondary to leadership development. The servant-empowering organization is not really focused on accomplishing projects, but growing leaders who can accomplish projects. Time invested in growing and equipping leaders is always valuable. Even if a temporary reduction in productivity occurs, it is better to invest in leadership development for the long-term success of the organization. Here are the painful lessons traditional leaders must learn to transition to a servant-empowering, team-based organization:

- *Mistakes will be made.* Leadership development demands the freedom to make mistakes. The goal of the organization is not to avoid mistakes, but to learn from mistakes. The more mistakes are made, the more opportunities for problem solving and continuous education emerge. Servant-empowering organizations do not penalize people for mistakes. They reward people for learning from their mistakes. A mistake-free environment is the fastest way to lose a competitive edge or to dull mission impact, because the organization ceases to be creative, innovative, and experimental.
- *Quality may suffer.* When "quest for quality" becomes "obsession for quality," the organization declines. Quality must sometimes be allowed to go down. Amateurs must be encouraged to take real initiative; rookies must be given an opportunity to take responsibility; laity must be given authority. People must be given the opportunity to be mediocre, so that they can evaluate their performance and learn to do better. True teams

are about gaining experience, apprenticing new leaders, and allowing newcomers to test their abilities.

- *Results may be slower in coming.* It may take longer to achieve success, but that success will be longer lasting and offer more assurance for future accomplishments. The organization must be patient. More time and money will be spent on embedding vision, developing integrity, training skills, and equipping teamwork *before* the organization sees much result in the mission market.

- *Gaps will emerge.* Internal organizational needs and external mission opportunities may go unaddressed for a time. This will be extremely uncomfortable, but the servant-empowering organization will always resist returning to the old habit of task groups and committees. It is better to live uncomfortably in the gaps than to deploy volunteers who are ill-equipped to function as a team and will soon burn out. That habit will make it even harder to invite newcomers into leadership, and it will make it nearly impossible to restore older veterans to healthy service.

For true teams to multiply, the organization must give priority to leadership development rather than to product development. If the organization persists in this transition and engrains leadership development as the fundamental habit of the organization, then more and more leaders will emerge, more and more teams will be deployed, and the momentum for organizational impact on the mission market will accelerate.

The story of team development begins with the story of leadership development. Fundamentally, team leaders are not appointed or elected. They never represent any faction or administrative unit of the larger organization. They emerge from the profound consensus of the organization around core values, beliefs, vision and mission. They emerge from the serious "spirituality" of the organization. They emerge as spiritually disciplined *individuals,* who can apply expectations for accountable spiritual disciplines on *a group.* They represent only their own passion and calling as it aligns to the overall vision and mission of the organization.

Characteristics of Team Leaders

Team leaders reveal certain characteristics, and in turn they mentor other leaders to have these same characteristics.[1]

- *Mission Attitude:* Team leaders have a "heartburst" for a particular mission market. They yearn to convey a specific experience of grace or a product of unique value that will better the lives of other people beyond

---

[1] I wrote at length about "true teams" in my book *Coaching Change* (Nashville: Abingdon Press, 1996).

the current organizational community. Even if their particular work has to do with nurturing or equipping members of the community, they see beyond the community itself to the potential for outreach in the larger world.

It is not surprising that the mission attitude is often associated with the personal experience of transformation or growth of the leader himself or herself. One only communicates what one has experienced. One conveys what one values most. The mission attitude is therefore aligned with the larger vision and mission of the organization and is shaped by the integrity of core values and beliefs. The mission attitude is the surest sign that teams are like droplets "sprayed" outward as the organizational wave strikes the mission market.

- *Work Ethic:* Team leaders are constantly learning. They research the mission market to be as sensitive and relevant as possible. They acquire or improve skills, deliberately taking themselves out of their normal comfort zones of content and learning methodology. They dare to experience what is personally distasteful or unsettling.

  "Hard work" means that they merge mission and lifestyle. They make no artificial separation between personal time and work time. They enjoy what they do and do what they enjoy. Every aspect of life is relevant to the pursuit and success of their mission. Team leaders generally abhor meetings because they waste time and suggest lack of trust. They tend to communicate "from the field" as work is "in progress" and to toil equally with other team members both to contribute to the outcome and to provide an example.

- *Constant Adaptability:* Team leaders both analyze and synthesize. They can study a problem and break it down into constituent pieces. They can then assemble a new perspective or a new approach that overcomes the problem. They do not follow incremental strategic plans. They are opportunists who can seize unexpected opportunities as they arise, abandoning what does not work without lament and embracing a new idea with zeal.

  Team leaders are *radically* pragmatic because at heart they are uncompromisingly absolutist. They treat the values, beliefs, vision, and mission as fixed points for behavior. They regard the policies of the organization as a sacred trust. They are scrupulous about executive limitations. Within those boundaries, however, they feel utterly free to innovate and experiment. They remain as indifferent to the offence other members of the organization take as they are passionate about the relevance experienced by the mission market. Their listening is not attuned to the timidity of their colleagues, but to the yearning of the people they seek to reach.

- *Persistence:* Team leaders are doggedly persistent. They may not be brilliant or charismatic. What attracts loyalty from their team and what gains credibility from the target public is their endurance and persistence in the face of persecution or resistance. They keep going, whether it is inches at a time or by leaps and bounds. Even when innumerable attempts have failed, they try again, adjusting tactics on the fly.

Team leaders are passionate about success, but do not demand instant gratification. Just as the organization understands that it may take time to grow the leaders for long-lasting and effective outreach, so also team leaders understand it may take time to grow the team members. "Out-reach" requires substantial "In-reach." They encourage mistakes, suffer occasional lapses in quality, and live in the gaps for the sake of even greater productivity by the team.

- *High Self-Esteem:* Team leaders believe they are winners, even when they lose. Failure does not depress them. They have strong egos and sometimes may be accused of arrogance. Yet only people who know they are beloved are really capable of true love. Team leaders do not need a great deal of recognition. They do not need public thanks, awards or medals. They do need the personal support of credible spiritual leaders in the organization who say "well done, good and faithful servant." Insofar as that "credible spiritual leader" is internalized by the voice of God, they are content to work in relative obscurity.

  This strong self-confidence or self-reliance should not be confused with mere individuality. Team leaders act independently because they are convinced that they deserve trust. The more trust is given, the more confident team leaders become. They welcome accountability if it is in the context of high trust and policy governance. They hate supervision and oversight that tries to tell them what to do or how to do it. Supervision is essentially demeaning to them, but accountability to the absolutes of spirituality fills them with pride.

This ideal picture of the team leader may be difficult for the organization to achieve. Part of the growth and training of team leaders is to help them develop those aspects of team leadership in which they are weakest. Nevertheless, these are the characteristics of the kind of leader who is both attracted to, and nurtured by, the servant-empowering organization.

The Contrast with Traditional Task Group Leaders

Just as traditional organizations tend to resist true teams, so also they tend to reject true team leaders. The qualities of a task group leader or committee chairperson are very different from those of a true team leader.

- *Employee Attitude:* Task group leaders and committee chairpersons are motivated by a responsibility to do a job, but not by a heartburst for a particular public. They respect the passion *of the company* for a purposeful mission, but implement that mission from a safe distance of skepticism. It is not their own passion. Most employees, and their middle management supervisors, have not personally been transformed by the benefits of the product they are offering to the public. They are hired to do a job or manage a work area, and they will do it as well as they can so long as it does *not* impinge on their private lives too much.

- *Maintenance Ethic:* Task group leaders and committee chairpersons are very committed to maintaining the current products or programs, but are not particularly dedicated to innovation or creativity. Once they are initially trained in existing procedures and strategies, they are not compelled to learn new things. Continuous learning is an "extra" that increases their workload, and innovation is a change that adds stress to their stable employment.

  The maintenance ethic does not mean that task group leaders and committee chairpersons do not work hard *when they are on the job,* but that they segment their private lives *from the job.* There is no merging of work and lifestyle. Task group leaders do not expect to enjoy what they do or to do what they enjoy. So long as the work is tolerable and does not seriously influence their life in general, they feel successful.

- *Institutional Loyalty:* Task group leaders and committee chairpersons are intensely loyal to their parent institution, but do not feel a strong obligation to the publics that institution serves. They value the products the company offers, but expect the public to appreciate and use those products. The public should adapt to the company; the company should not have to adapt to the public. Declining outreach, influence, or "sales" always indicate that there is something wrong with the public, not with the product.

  The defensiveness on the part of task group leaders and committee chairpersons has a double significance. Externally, task group leaders and committee chairpersons regard expectations for change as a kind of personal affront. They conclude that "we don't count" or that "everything we used to do must be valueless." Internally, they become increasingly needy for affirmation. They must always be thanked verbally or in writing; honored for seniority or service; or awarded perks for achievement. Paradoxically, this defensiveness means that the primary reason task group leaders and committee chairpersons *leave* an organization is because they were *obsessively loyal to the institution in the first place.*

- *Control:* Task group leaders and committee chairpersons treat management prescriptively as a form of control. They want to tell people what to do and how to do it. They recruit people to implement strategies that are not their own, expect little deviation from approved strategic plans, and claim the right to evaluate results without necessarily consulting the workers. In short, they list everything people can or should do and reserve the right to approve or disapprove of any extras.

The more defensive task group leaders and committee chairpersons become, the more control becomes heavy-handed, mean-hearted, and dictatorial. If defensiveness is assuaged through lower demands for change and higher expressions of appreciation, control may become lighter, kinder, and permissive. That is not a sign of servant empowerment, however, but of organizational surrender of mission attitude. The company will become happier, and for a time productivity will plateau or even increase, but then decline will become even steeper as changes in the mission market outstrip organizational adaptability.

- *High Self-Interest:* Task group leaders and committee chairpersons will make incredible sacrifices *if organizational goals and personal self-interest coincide.* If organizational change or expansion promises higher rewards, opportunities for promotion, greater influence, or deeper personal satisfaction, then task group leaders and committee chairpersons will invest overtime, temporarily sacrifice income, risk unpopularity, and take other risks on behalf of the organization. The appeal, however, is not to their pride in the spirituality or mission of the organization, or their concern to benefit the public, but to their own self-interest.

Confidence is placed in the hierarchy (the board of directors, the senior pastor, or the CEO), to whom the task group leaders and committee chairpersons look for prescriptive direction. They expect to be told what to do. They will subsequently share in the glory of success and blame the hierarchy in the pain of defeat. This is not self-confidence, but dependence on supervision. It is in their self-interest *not to be free.*

It becomes obvious why traditional organizations tend to reject true team leaders, and why true team leaders tend to avoid traditional organizations. This contrast paints a black-and-white picture to teach the principles of team leadership, but the truth is that many leaders are caught in the grey area in between. With the right encouragement and with focused training, many task group leaders and committee chairpersons *might become* true team leaders. For them to flourish, however, the whole atmosphere, spirituality, or organizational model will have to change. True team leaders will either force a larger organizational change for board and management, or they will leave. The change to board and management will be explained in subsequent chapters.

True Teams

The description of a "true team" necessarily follows the explanation of "true team leadership." This reversal of traditional organizational explanations is deliberate, because it illustrates the essential difference in servant-empowering organization. Servant-empowering organizations are not primarily focused on *program development* but on *leadership development.* To be more productive, they develop leaders. They do not develop programs to be productive. The "true team" is as much a circle of mentoring to grow and multiply leaders as it is a unit of productivity to accomplish work.

Leadership development and productivity are merged in the apprenticing experience.

True Team Design

Therefore, the qualities of a true team leader are mirrored in the design of the true team. The accountability of the team is assured so long as the team leader is accountable to the spirituality of the entire organization. The team leader embeds the core values, beliefs, vision, and mission into the team members. The team leader focuses the ends policies and procedures of the organization on team activity, and helps design the executive limitations that will keep the team from contradicting the values and beliefs, or from sidetracking from the vision and mission.

The image of the organizational "wave" spraying out "droplets" of water reveals the essential unity of the team and the organization. The internal constitution of the droplet is the same as the internal constitution of the wave. The droplets, or teams, can stick, drip, and merge because this unity is intentionally and even aggressively pursued. Droplets have the potential of becoming waves; waves only fulfill their purpose by spraying forth droplets. Only in this way can the shoreline be sculpted, and the mission market be influenced.

The team leader handpicks the team members. Team members are not elected or appointed, and they certainly do not represent various other factions or groups in the organization in the manner of committee participation. The team leader invites each team member to serve. The accountability of the team member is to the team and only to the team.

Elements of a True Team

Team members will be invited to join the team using five criteria that mirror the qualities of team leadership. They are "leaders-in-process." Mentoring is as much a purpose of team life as accomplishing work. The diagram below uses the image of a molecule of water to describe the elements of a true team. Note that each element in the molecule has "connectivity" with other molecules (or teams). These are the ways in which team droplets stick, drip, and merge with other teams.

- *Spirituality:* Team members all think and behave in reference to the spirituality of the organization. They share the same core values, beliefs, vision, and mission. This parallels the mission attitude of the team leader, which has been born out of this same spirituality. The more intentionally this milieu of spirituality is embedded in the team member, the more likely a new team leader will emerge. This spirituality will be revealed *behaviorally* in the total life and lifestyle of the team member. Team life and individual life are not segmented. They are one.

  The spirituality of the team members *connects* with any organizational gathering that defines, refines, and celebrates the spirituality that is the

The True Team

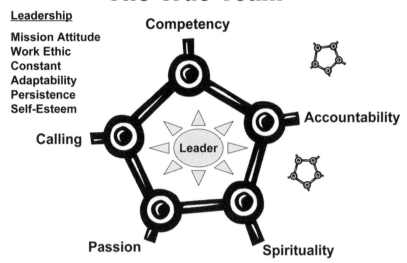

Leadership

Mission Attitude
Work Ethic
Constant
Adaptability
Persistence
Self-Esteem

Competency

Accountability

Calling

Leader

Passion

Spirituality

foundation of trust. In church, for example, the team *connects* with weekly worship, daily shared devotions, and other corporate acts of meditation. Although worship has multiple layers of meaning, the *organizational function* of worship is to connect teams with the spirituality of the organization. In other nonprofit or corporate organizations, the team *connects* with any annual gathering or corporate celebration. These gatherings are not just about morale, but about embedding the spirituality of the organization in the teams, and modeling the spiritual behavior of team leaders for team members.

• *Passion:* Team members all share a common enthusiasm for the particular mission of the team, which is aligned with the overall mission of the organization. This is not just an interest. It is a passion. Team members may not immediately have the skill, or the quality of skill, to do the work of the team; but if they have the passion, they will be ready to learn whatever they need to learn. Team members must be *thrilled* to be invited onto the team. The thrill or excitement of the team mission is what compels them to merge work and lifestyle.

   The passion of the team members *connects* with the persistence of the organization, and therefore with any agency within or beyond the organization that can offer leverage to make even the smallest advance toward the mission goal. It is particularly important to connect passion with persistence in the context of research and development. Countercultural organizations, such as the church, are prone to give up too early on worship, outreach, volunteer recruitment, or technological change because it is too hard, too stressful, too laborious, or too expensive–*unless* their teams are driven by such a passion that they painstakingly search for any and every opportunity for growth.

- *Calling:* Team members all share a strong sense of calling to the mission of the team. This is more than a passion. It is a compulsion or urgency to follow a higher purpose that is at once ennobling and dangerous. It is a response to something greater than oneself, and even greater than the organization. This higher purpose shapes the vocation of the individual, in which team participation is relevant as a means to an end. Executive limitations on coordination or cooperation can "block and guide" the means to pursue the calling, but the team is free to devise its own way to achieve results.

  Therefore, the calling of the team members *connects* with the adaptability of the organization and with any agency that helps the organization be sensitive to the mission market. Calling allows team members to free themselves from the "sacred cows" of tactics and strategies, and empowers them to understand emerging microcultures and adjust the content and delivery of the "product." Effectiveness and efficiency become possible when team members surrender to a higher purpose. They will avoid becoming sidetracked in the "worship of idols" and focus on what ultimately concerns the organization.

- *Competency:* Team members all share a commitment to constantly improving competencies. Individual team members may join a team because of spirituality, passion, and calling; but they cannot stay in a team unless they are committed to learn and interface skills to achieve the mission results. They are in a quest for quality, but unlike traditional organizations the standards of quality are set internally by the team and are unique to the team mission. Competency is not just about skills, but about the collaborative use of skills to achieve common goals.

  The competencies of team members for specific skills and overall teamwork *connect* with the work ethic of the organization. Teams seek out any agency or opportunity for continuing education and training. Executive limitations can "block and guide" certain educational choices, but the team is free to go anywhere, bring in any consultant, read any literature, and partner with any agency (crossing boundaries of sector, culture, and learning methodology) to achieve the competency necessary for mission results. Basic training within the company is not enough. Upgrades obtained beyond the company, within the mission market, are crucial. Teams, like software, upgrade to a new "version" of competence constantly.

- *Accountability:* Team members all commit to accountability based on peer-to-peer evaluation. They hold one another accountable for spirituality that is aligned with organizational core values and convictions and for passion that is aligned with organizational vision and mission. The team leader, in turn, will be accountable to the organization as a whole for his or her ability to guide the team within the ends policies and process policies of organizational governance. Similarly, the team members hold one another accountable for their quest for quality and mission results. The team leader, in turn, will be accountable to the organization as a whole for the executive limitations that protect safety, guide continuous learning, and coordinate action.

Therefore, the accountability of the team *connects* with the self-esteem of the leader, every member of the team, and the overall pride of the organization. Morale is never based on privilege, but on discipline. The higher the standard of accountability (equally applied and expected among all teams and team members) the higher the self-esteem of every individual participant in the organization. This contributes to the credibility of the whole organization within the mission market. "Spiritual discipline" applies not only to churches, but to all organizations in the emerging world. Organizations that are explicit in their expectations and assertive in holding members accountable for behavior and policy not only increase the productivity of the organization but also expand the connectivity of the organization.

Conclusion

Every true team, whatever its unique mission purpose, functions around these principles. Like droplets of water, this common function is what allows them to "stick, drip, and merge." If we could freeze each droplet into a crystalline form, we would find remarkable similarity in the replicated structure of each team, but also uniqueness as each team shapes itself relevantly to the mission market. If we could merge these crystallized teams into a larger "iceberg," we would see that three-fifths of the team structure is submerged or hidden from immediate notice (i.e. spirituality, passion, and calling). Only two-fifths of the team "mass" is overtly visible (i.e. competency and accountability). Yet whether in liquid or crystalline form, and whether small or large, the true team is an irresistible force.

The Dynamic of Board and Management

The Visionary Board

Empowering Management

The Dynamic of Board and Management

The second fundamental dynamic in the servant-empowering organization is the fluid movement between board and management. Remember, a "dynamic" is a movement in the life of an organization that is predictable in its occurrence, but unpredictable in its result. That is to say, it is an organizational piece that functions with predictable principles, but is also free to create, innovate, and explore in new and unpredictable ways.

Organizational life demands some form of direction and persuasion. It demands some instrument for targeting and channeling energy. In simple organizations, such as a true team, "targeting" can be done by the team leader and "channeling" can be done by the tactical consensus of the team members. In more complex organizations, the individual leader can no longer "target" all of the activities of the organization, and the members of any single team can no longer "channel" energy through tactical consensus. If they attempt to do so, mission results will suffer as the organization turns inward to spend more time on oversight than productivity.

Bottom-up Growth for Success

What drives the dynamic of board and management is not really "complexity." What drives this dynamic is success. The more successful an organization becomes in achieving long-lasting mission results, the more urgent it is to develop the dynamic of board and management. Organizations naturally grow "bottom-up" rather than "top-down." *First,* there are consensus and teams; *then* there are boards and management. The very success of teams, emerging from a common spirituality, eventually demands a more sophisticated dynamic to target and channel the increasing energies of the organization. Success *probably* leads to more complexity, but not *necessarily.* It is not the complexity, but the success of the organization that precipitates the need for a board and for management.

Traditional Top-down Growth versus Entrepreneurial Growth

Traditional organizations of modernity (in contrast to ancient and medieval organization) have it backward. This is a result of the Newtonian, mechanistic, or as some say "scientistic," ordering of the universe into hierarchies of species that interact in external relations. Modern organizations start with boards and management, and then recruit, appoint, nominate, or elect "sub-sets" of organizational life that are charged with implementing the tasks imposed by the hierarchy.

- The classic "startup" strategy for modernity has been to incorporate a board, develop a management strategy, and then, when the supervisory body is ready, appoint the task groups and committees to implement the agenda. In the same way, nonprofit agencies in the United States *first* obtained their 501c status; and denominations in the Western world *first* imposed denominational polity on a newly forming congregation. "Top-down" means imposing a straight jacket of uniformity that will make it easy for a board and management to control everything that goes on.
- The classic "startup" strategy for ancient and postmodern culture is to *first* form a true team that identifies a spiritual consensus as the primary vehicle of accountability. Teams resist any imposed structural uniformity and, if necessary, operate underneath or at the margins of polity and jurisprudence. As the organization becomes successful in obtaining mission results, multiplies teams, and presumably grows in complexity, the organization customizes board and management to help target and channel the energies of the organization for maximum efficiency and effectiveness.

The latter strategy is called "entrepreneurial" and is often criticized by advocates of the classic modern strategy as being too risky.

What modernity has forgotten is that the ability to risk lies at the core of successful organizational life. Organizations that have not arisen from risk will not be able to undertake risk. They will simply conform to the expectations of society in the present, and be unable to adapt to the expectations of society in the future. When you look back on the cultural changes and organizational innovations of history, whether in the church, or politics, or industry, or any other sector of public life, all great organizations emerged from the shadows of controversy and legality.

Board and Management Dynamic

The metaphor of "waves sculpting the shoreline" is just as useful in describing the dynamic of board and management as it is in describing the dynamic of consensus and team. Think not just of a single wave spraying droplets of water against the shoreline, but of the relentless onslaught of waves showering the shoreline with droplets of water. Success in shaping the shoreline is influenced by the regularity, intensity, angle of impact and other factors of water in motion. When the wave metaphor is applied to organizational life, and the "waves" are seen not as "acts of God" but as human endeavors, these factors become the focus of board and management.

Here is the same chart from the previous chapter, now highlighting the role of board and management in the servant-empowering organization:

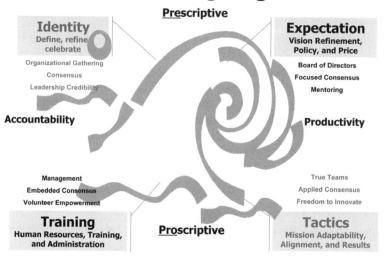

The Empowering Organization

Prescriptive

Identity
Define, refine,
celebrate

Organizational Gathering

Consensus

Leadership Credibility

Expectation
Vision Refinement,
Policy, and Price

Board of Directors

Focused Consensus

Mentoring

Accountability

Productivity

Management

Embedded Consensus

Volunteer Empowerment

True Teams

Applied Consensus

Freedom to Innovate

Training
Human Resources, Training,
and Administration

Proscriptive

Tactics
Mission Adaptability,
Alignment, and Results

- The board positions itself at the crest of the wave, or, expanding the view, at an elevation above the turgid sea. Their role is to define the expectation for change. Just how is the shoreline to be sculpted? Just how should the mission market be influenced? How should the regularity, intensity, and angle of impact of organizational life be adjusted to fulfill the vision and mission that is the consensus of the organization?
- The management positions itself beneath the wave, or, expanding the view, at the uneven surface below the turgid water. Their role is to understand the contours of the emerging mission market and to provide the training and support that will achieve success. Just how do teams need to be equipped? What resources will they need to adapt to new circumstances? Just how can they stay on line for maximum impact?

The answers are urgent for the success of the overall organizational mission. It is not realistic to simultaneously be at the crest of the wave and the bottom of the wave. These are distinct functions for distinct pieces of the organization. If either fails, the consensus will begin to break down; the waves will lose regularity, intensity, and impact; and the teams that emerge as droplets sprayed at the mission market will no longer "stick, drip, and merge." The sea may be more turgid than before, but it will be chaos and nothing else.

Conclusion

The dynamic of board and management is to bring order to that chaos. Board and management do not need to "stir things up." That will happen through the dynamic of consensus and team and as the spirituality of the organization confronts the reality of the world. Teams and team leaders will cause things to happen. Consensus interacting with culture will bring about change. Eventually the very impact of consensus and teams will create chaos. It is the dynamic of board and management that will order that chaos, imposing predictability, intentionality, and purpose.

The Visionary Board

The whole purpose of a board of directors in the servant-empowering organization is to position the organization for success fifteen years into the future, and determine what price the organization should pay to get there. They do this by establishing ends policies, process policies, and executive limitations on management and by personifying the identity of the organization in their work and lifestyles. All the activity of a board of directors rotates around the two basic activities of "focusing" and "mentoring." Fundamentally, the board asks and answers the question: *If we remain faithful to who we are, what should we reasonably expect to happen?*

When this concept of visionary board is applied to the church, then the whole purpose of a board is clear. The board of a church discerns where Jesus will be fifteen years down the road in mission, and counts the cost of discipleship that will become necessary to join Jesus there. The fundamental conviction of the church is that Jesus is alive, active, and pursuing God's mission in the world. Their job is to catch up with him. The board needs to decide what the Christian mission will look like fifteen years into the future and decide what price they will have to pay to join Jesus there. That is what it means to be faithful to the identity of the church.

The Visionary Board's Activities

Unlike traditional, modern boards, servant-empowering boards do not do management. They do not develop and monitor budgets, read and approve reports, develop and oversee tasks, hire and fire personnel, or negotiate contracts. As we shall see, in the servant-empowering organization these responsibilities will be entrusted to a gifted few who will manage the regular operations of the organization.

Traditional modern organizations, however, waste time doing all of these things. They create redundant levels of management to oversee and supervise task groups and committees, immersing themselves in the details of daily, monthly, annual business. This means that they spend very little time doing what matters most to the future of the organization. They spend no time envisioning the future and positioning the organization to impact that future. They spend no time modeling organizational identity and mentoring organizational members to embed that identity in their routines and lifestyles. Before long, traditional modern organizations find themselves losing momentum. They have no direction, less impact, and few leaders. Servant-empowering boards focus and mentor. These are the key elements in visioning.

Traditional modern leaders regard servant-empowering boards with a mixture of admiration and skepticism. They do not understand the direct connection between vision and trust. Servant-empowering boards can risk investing all their time in visioning because they create and maintain high trust. Visions only emerge in an atmosphere of trust; trust only thrives when visioning is a priority. Traditional organizations cannot be visionary, because they function in an atmosphere of distrust. No matter how hard they try to "appreciate" employees, their very obsession with approvals and supervision reveals their bias that employees, left to themselves, are fundamentally untrustworthy. They will inevitably do something stupid, illegal, or expensive. Similarly, no matter how much employees declare admiration for management, their skepticism of leadership remains. They are unclear about the positive core values and beliefs of the organization, and highly doubtful that their leaders personify it.

Ironically, the inability to understand the direct connection between vision and trust is most apparent in the church. The church laments that there is no vision among church leadership, but fails to realize that the root cause is that there is no trust among church membership. Or the church laments that membership has been fractured by rival factions, but fails to realize that the root cause is that there is no vision among the leaders.

- *When there is no vision, the organization fights itself.*
  The reactionary thinking of modern church life is that internal fighting requires the immersion of leaders in management. Take control! This only accelerates dysfunction. Leaders are drawn down into more and more meetings, obsessively maintaining harmony in the church, and nobody guides the long-term future of the church. The church becomes one happy family largely irrelevant to the mission market.

- *When there is no trust, the organization loses itself.*
  The reactionary thinking of modern church life is that confusion about purpose requires strategic planning and the intervention of a hierarchy. Take control! Leaders are drawn down into even more meetings, brainstorming ways to survive as an institution, and nobody is held accountable for their actual behavior. The church is driven by whatever agenda is politically correct or financially lucrative this year.

Servant-empowering organizations understand this connection between vision and trust. Because the board invests so much time envisioning the faithful future, organizational teams can be given so much trust. Because the teams have a reason to trust one another, they can free their board to envision the future.

Visionary Board's Functions

Focus the Future

The first function of a servant-empowering board is to define expectations so that the organization can reasonably measure results. This is what it means to "focus the future." Expectation is not wishful thinking. It is more like geometric progression. Draw a line between two fixed points of *conviction* (core values and beliefs) and *purpose* (vision and mission), and then extend that line to intersect culture. The board envisions the positive changes or negative threats that will emerge from that projected point of intersection, and readies the organization to either seize the opportunities or defend itself against the liabilities.

It sounds simple enough. Picture one line between two points, and extend it across a specific period of time reaching from the past, through the present, and into the future. The point of intersection is the point of mission. That is where results will be measurable. Looking back, the board should be able to see a direct alignment with their core values and beliefs, motivating vision and heartburst mission. Looking ahead, the board should be able to anticipate specific results (positive or negative) that will result from that alignment.

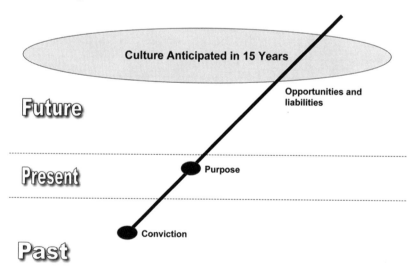

In fact, the work of the board is considerably more difficult. If it were as simple as that, one would not really need a board. A single visionary team leader could do it. The reality is different.

- *The "fixed points" are less permanent than we think.*

  The organization's conviction about core values and beliefs will evolve over time. This does *not* mean that the core values and beliefs are not true, but that our grasp of truth in the midst of existence will shift. Why will it shift? Leaders and members of the organization will change and grow, viewing the truth from fresh perspectives. Since life is essentially unpredictable and uncontrollable, joy and tragedy will transform and reshape our values and beliefs.

  The organization's clarity of purpose (vision and mission) will also evolve over time. Again, this does *not* mean that motivating vision and heartburst mission are unwarranted, but that our experience of vision and mission will shift. Visions may expand or contract; missions may be multiplied or refined. In the context of spirituality, in which visions are revealed rather than created, God may reveal a new thing.

- *Culture is constantly fragmenting and diversifying.*

  The organization does not have one public, but many publics. Every one of them is experiencing both evolutionary and revolutionary change. If you blink, the world is different. Mobility and communication in the global economy presents exponentially increasing opportunities and hazards.

  This means that the organizational trajectory does not intersect with one culture, but with innumerable cultures. These cultures are themselves in movement. They are not static. They may drift across the organizational trajectory, or even ram the organizational trajectory. The opportunities for the organization to become sidetracked or deflected off course abound.

The actual chart for the visionary board of a servant-empowering organization looks something like this:

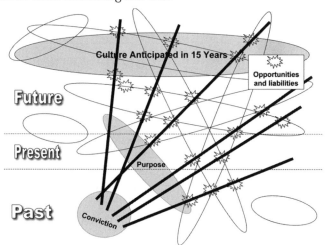

This does not mean that the organization will take dramatic turns, or reverse direction 180 degrees, and abrogate its fundamental conviction and purpose. It does mean that the organization will inevitably alter direction in varying small degrees, and these choices must be made judiciously. Unless the board is careful in making these choices, the organization may well be subject to sharp turns that contradict its conviction and purpose as it is pressured and impacted by culture after culture. This is a more complex situation. A single leader can't do this. It requires a visionary board.

TRADITIONAL BOARD FUNCTIONS

The visionary board focuses the future for the organization. Traditional management boards do not do this. Traditional boards invest most of their time supervising tasks, moving back and forth along the line between conviction and purpose. They rarely look into the future. They are remarkably ignorant of the emerging complexity of culture in the mission market. They are easily blindsided, sidetracked, or blocked from their mission—and sometimes do not even know it!

The traditional organization may be *blocked* by culture.

In this case, the inability of the board to evolve conviction and purpose, and the diversification of culture, causes the organization to become irrelevant. It is deflected from mission, and shrinks in upon itself.

In the case of a church, the congregation retreats into the past, the congregation ages, and chaplaincy attitudes protect membership privileges.

The traditional organization may be *diffused* by culture.

In this case, the obsession of the board with supervision and management allows outside forces to co-opt or sidetrack the energy of the organization for other purposes. Eventually the organization is broken up and lost.

In the case of the church, the organization sidetracks to become a social agency, political advocacy, heritage museum, or units of other sociopolitical agendas.

The traditional organization may be *destroyed* by culture.

In this case, the board's insensitivity to the future allows some crisis or catastrophe to overtake the organization. This may be a legal, moral, or financial crisis.

In the case of the church, the organization is embroiled in some public policy debate, litigation, or moral debacle that undermines credibility. The assets are assigned elsewhere by the civil court. The organization simply ceases to exist.

Servant-empowering organizations avoid these dangers and function very differently from traditional boards. This is why servant-empowering organizations have greater longevity and impact. They are less likely to stray dramatically from their core conviction and purpose, and more likely to change the world.

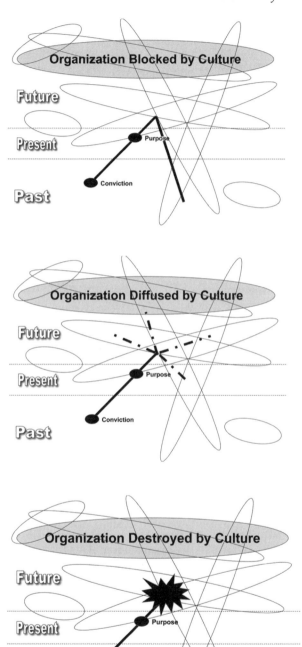

Traditional, incremental, top-down strategic planning does not remedy the underlying problem of traditional boards. Yes, strategic planning does look into the future, but it tends to assume that cultural change will be slow and controllable and that the same basic tactics that worked in the past just need minor adjustments to be successful in the future. Strategic planning tends to imagine the future using the templates of the past. Servant-empowering organizations demand that visionary boards function differently.

REFINE THE VISION

The visionary board invests significant time exploring the emerging cultural diversity and cross-cultural chaos. They constantly examine, and sometimes initiate, demographic research. Their scrutiny penetrates layers of detail:

- Basic demography (age, race, income, occupation, family structure, relationship, housing, mobility, and religious affiliation);
- Lifestyle segment (cultural left, right, and middle defining attitudes, habits, mores, environments, and trends);
- Affinity groups (shared enthusiasms, addictions, contexts, and sensibilities).

Visionary boards want to know the cultural *detail* and *movement* that fills their primary mission market. They need to understand the complexity of the future that confronts their organization. Their vision of the emerging future is transformed like a prism bends light. Previously the board simply recognized a *single* culture. Now their vision is fractured or "bent" to recognize multiple "colors" of culture or a multitude of interacting microcultures.

They will add to this research constant dialogue with senior organizational leaders in social service, health care, business (research and development, manufacturing, retail, marketing), government (policy development and law enforcement), academic, and religious organizations. This dialogue will take place with local, regional, national, and international leaders within the anticipated sphere of influence of their organizational mission. They will talk with other visionary boards in other servant-empowering organizations to trade insights and ideas.

As the visionary board looks outward toward the emerging mission market, they are specifically looking for points of intersection where their organizational mission and the emerging publics are singularly relevant to each other. This point of relevance may be positive or negative. Positive relevance means an opportunity to leverage change that reshapes the microculture and has a cascading effect to influence events within that microculture and with other microcultures. Negative relevance means an impending crisis in which some microculture or movement of microcultures might damage or undermine their organizational mission.

To decide *which* intersections to cross and *which* intersections to avoid, the board must not only look outward to the mission market, but also inward to its own identity and purpose. The conversation about "who we are" and "where should we go" never ceases within the life of a visionary board. The visionary board is the collective "intuition" of the servant-empowering organization. They lead by their instinct as much as by their future projections. Traditional boards may "look inward" by surveying membership opinion or soliciting membership voting, but servant-empowering boards know that is futile. They are chosen as leaders because their collective "instinct" is trusted. They cannot flee from the responsibility of making difficult or ambiguous choices about the future of the organization by putting it off to a vote. *They decide* the trajectory of the organization.

Visionary boards refine the vision through constant meditation, as individuals and as a group. They continually reflect on the sacred texts related to their core values and bedrock beliefs. They ponder the origin and significance of their motivating purpose. They consider the wisdom and insight of previous organizational leaders, or leaders of similar organizations. Most importantly, they open themselves to the spirit that has called them to service in the first place. In the context of a Christian church, this means that the board is, foremost in the organization, to search scripture, reflect theologically, pay attention to apostolic history, and pray fervently. A board member who misses regular worship, or who is undisciplined about spiritual life, is not only hurting his or her own soul, but betraying the congregation as a leader.

When we consider that *all* organizations have a "spirituality," it becomes clear that any board in any public sector (even business) must continually refine the organizational vision through intense meditation. Even so-called secular organizations have a spiritual center that is the source for the intuition of the board. It is their life-force or reason for living. If board members are no longer in touch with that center of spirituality, they can no longer have reliable instincts to chart the trajectory of the organization and to choose which intersections to cross or avoid. Fundamentally, visions are revealed. To remain aligned to that vision and follow that vision, the board must continually return to their ultimate concern. God (however the organization names the infinite) gave the vision and can shift the vision. The board cannot control it, but they must keep up with it.

DEVELOP THE POLICIES

Policy governance is the practical outcome of refining the vision. The visionary board ensures that the organization keeps up with the vision, and rigorously aligns all of its activities with the vision, by developing policies (boundaries and limitations) that keep the organization on course. The board does not do management in the sense of assigning, monitoring, and evaluating tasks. It manages in the sense of guiding the organization through strategically devised policies.

I discussed policy governance in a previous chapter. The board refines the vision by establishing "ends policies" that identify the anticipated positive relevance of the organization for personal and social change in any given microculture. It further embeds specific organizational habits for the discernment, design, implementation, and evaluation of *any* initiative. These are "process policies." They do not specify any particular initiative, but simply demand that *any* initiative must be shaped by certain organizational habits as a result of shared consensus over values, beliefs, vision, and mission. Finally, the board places specific "executive limitations" on those who do manage activities, in order to "block and guide" for safety and confidentiality, continuing education, and coordinate action. These are "proscriptions" that simply specify the handful of strategic options leaders in the organization may *not* do. Policy governance is a way to free the board from oppressive top-down task management and provide a vehicle for reasonable, measurable trust that turns the creative energies of staff and volunteers loose on the mission market.

The visionary board must resist any and all temptations to be drawn into the task management of the organization. For people brought up in modernity, and the typical organizational thinking of the post-Enlightenment Western world, this can be very difficult. Boards constantly want to look at financial statements, read reports, approve and disapprove things, and generally meddle in matters that are not their affair. They are constantly tempted to think that *control* is their job, when it is not. *Vision* is their job. The more they control, the more they distrust. And the more they distrust, the more obscure the vision becomes. The more obscure the vision becomes, the more the instinct and intuition of the board is dulled. There will be a place to monitor financial statements and oversee teams, but it is not here. In the metaphor of the wave, a visionary board does not place itself in the midst of the spray as the wave impacts culture. The board places itself on the crest for a clear view of sea and sand.

COUNT THE COST

The visionary board decides what price the organization must pay to be effective at the point of mission. These points of mission, of course, are the positive and negative intersections between organizational trajectory and microcultures. To seize the one or avoid the other, the visionary board must anticipate what the cost will be to the organization, so that the organization can start preparing itself now. The board may not be involved in the multitude of specific tasks in organizational life (programs, personnel, resources, etc.), but it *must* be involved in making strategic decisions that ready the organization for the opportunities and challenges of the future.

This is a form of "risk management." The visionary board decides what is at stake for the organization in the future. They decide what the organization must risk, and what they must *not* risk, to impact the emerging mission market. What must change? What must be protected? What is sacred to organizational integrity, and what is dispensable? What is necessary to have the greatest positive influence on the mission market of the future? What is faithful to the origin and purpose of the organization, and what is unfaithful? These are the questions the servant-empowering board addresses.

Once the visioning board discerns the positive or negative relevance of the organization to the emerging microcultures of the future, they decide what must be sacrificed or acquired to address the challenge. In Christian terminology, the board discerns where Jesus will be in future mission and counts the cost of discipleship demanded to join Jesus there. The visioning board determines the cost of discipleship, or the price of success, in the following order:

- *Heritage Cost:* These are changes in traditional organizational practice. Every organization develops a history. Even startup organizations just three years old settle into comfortable patterns and norms. The board must decide what price the organization must pay to change normative ways of thinking, learning, and doing. For a church, this represents change in local or denominational heritage. For a business, this represents change of familiar technologies. Removing an outdated, but familiar, telephone system is akin to removing pews from the traditional sanctuary. Visionary boards slay sacred cows.

- *Attitude Cost:* These are changes in perspective toward individuals, groups, movements, and behavior. Every organization develops hidden or overt biases and prejudices, and sometimes these are have been justified by multiple layers of rationalization. The board must decide which fundamental assumptions should be challenged or maintained, and differentiate between the prejudices of staff and volunteers versus the expectations legitimately aligned to core values. Challenging stereotypes about sexuality, age, race, language, and other perspectives on the world can be painful. Visionary boards confront prejudice.

- *Lifestyle Cost:* These are changes in personal habits and holistic behavior. Every organization condones staff and volunteer lifestyles to certain, often ill-defined, points. Limits always exist even when the organization officially declares indifference to lifestyle. As work and lifestyle merge in the servant-empowering organization, visionary boards must determine key lifestyle expectations that impact organizational credibility in mission. It makes no sense for the organization to value health, and allow team leaders to be overweight. It makes no sense for a church to leverage mission among the urban poor and allow the pastor to drive a sports car. Visionary boards intrude on the private lives of staff and volunteers.

- *Personnel Cost:* These are changes in staff and volunteer training and deployment. Every organization develops personnel to be as effective and efficient as possible. However, as the mission market changes and new opportunities and crises are anticipated, visionary boards must see the bigger picture for hiring, firing, training, and redeploying personnel. This does not mean they are involved in the details of job description and support packages, but that they foresee how personnel will be required to address the emerging future. Visionary boards anticipate leadership needs.
- *Organizational Cost:* These are changes in corporate structure and accountability. Every organization develops a system of shared work-load and accountability to design, implement, and evaluate tactics. As the mission market changes, the efficient structure today is no longer effective tomorrow. This does not mean that the board is involved in the management of programs or the process of accountability for all the teams. They foresee how pieces of the structure are more or less useful and how measurements of success may evolve in the future. Visionary boards reconfigure the organizational model.
- *Property Cost:* These are changes in location and facility. Every organization will locate itself geographically or digitally where it can most effectively reach the mission market. It establishes a facility, whether it be a physical building or a cyber Web site, and uses technologies, whether hardware or software. Visionary boards make the big decisions to relocate or reequip the organizational headquarters and product delivery systems. Nothing is sacred about property—even for a church. All that is sacred is mission and mission effectiveness. The location, facility, and technology are means to an end. Visionary boards position the organization for maximum mission impact.
- *Financial Cost:* These are changes in financial priorities, fund-raising, and investment. Every organization shapes a budget, gathers income, and invests money for future use. The priorities for that budget, the methods to gather income, and the nature and size of portfolios for investment will change as the mission evolves. Visionary boards give broad direction to the managers as to how money will be raised, used, and stored. This does not mean that the board is involved in the detail of monitoring finance, but that they give direction to the financial priorities of the organization. Visionary boards set the standard for stewardship.

Visionary boards manage risk in the order of priority outlined above. They start counting the cost of discipleship by considering the price of change in heritage, attitude, and lifestyle; proceed to set the price of change regarding personnel and structure; and only at the end consider the cost for mission relevance in property and financial change. If the organization is ready to pay the price of effective mission through changed heritage, attitude, and lifestyle, then changes in personnel and structure will be less traumatic, and changes in property and finance will be much less intimidating.

We can see the obvious "temptation" in risk management to become more immersed in the details of task management. Visionary boards must be very careful to resist that temptation. They are only interested in personnel, structure, property, and finance in regard to the *big strategic moves* for the organization. They resist involvement in decisions to fire a secretary, close an office, renovate a room, or meet an annual deficit–but they take responsibility for the big decisions to insist that all staff become bilingual, or to initiate a new trajectory of mission, or to relocate or build on another site of ministry, or to obtain a multi-million dollar loan. Visionary boards make the big strategic moves as a part of the "risk management" of the organization, but they are not involved in the daily or even annual business.

Mentor the Membership

The second function of a servant-empowering board is to personify expectations so that the organization can multiply trusted leaders. This is what it means to "mentor the membership." Board members see the hidden potential in people and invest time in their personal, professional, and missional growth. To take responsibility for the "big picture," board members must immerse themselves in the "little people." They are the connecting link between vision refinement and leadership development.

The visionary board members are the "spiritual leaders" of the organization. This is obvious in a church. It is equally true, albeit more subtle, in organizations of other kinds. The board leads through the credibility or authenticity of its board members and their ability to mature members of the organization to become the leaders of the future.

MODEL BEHAVIOR

Each member of a visionary board personifies the core values, beliefs, vision, and mission that together form the spirituality, foundation of trust, and consensus of the organization. If any newcomer or observer wants to understand what the organization is really about, all they need to do is shadow a member of the board every minute for twenty-four hours; and they will see the organization revealed in the behavior of the board member.

It is more urgent for the board members to align themselves to the core value, beliefs, vision, and mission of the organization than for the average member of the organization. If members are expected to behave in a certain way, stake their lives on specific beliefs, surrender to a motivating vision, and single-mindedly pursue a strategic mission...then it is doubly important for the board member to do this.

Behavioral modeling on the part of the board member parallels the vision refinement of the board as a whole. Each individual board member must be clear about his or her roots in the identity of the organization and personal calling as a leader. He or she draws a straight-line trajectory between these two points and extends it into his or her own personal future. He or she anticipates how his or her own career will intersect with positive or negative relevance with the lives of other individuals and with the movement of other microcultures. What the board does for the organization, the individual models for organizational members. He or she helps individuals clarify their own roots and their own personal missions and coaches them to align their missions to the corporate spirituality.

The outward/inward focus of vision refinement is revealed in the individual behavior of board members. In a sense, they have two lists of people with whom they regularly plan lunch. On the one hand, they regularly dine with other servant-empowering organizational leaders in other public sectors to trade insights about the mission market fifteen years away. On the other hand, they regularly dine with individual members of the organization, at whatever level of office or involvement, to help them define their own integrity and purpose in relation to the organization. Board members spend less time in meetings and more time in relationships.

GUIDE SPIRITUAL LIFE

Each member of the visionary board demonstrates and teaches the "spiritual life." The application of this principle to churches may be obvious, but remember that all organizations are "spiritual" and therefore all board members are "spiritual leaders." They are self-disciplined about structuring their lives around the core values, beliefs, vision, and mission of the organization.

Once again, the behavior of the board as a whole with the entire body is paralleled by the individual board members. The board exercises discipline through policy governance, and the individual board members organize their lives to demonstrate the same self-discipline for ends, processes, and executive limitations. They are clear about their own personal missions, personal habits of thought and decision-making, and proscriptive "Thou Shalt Not's" for daily living within and beyond the workplace.

One expects board members in a church, for example, to model and teach self-disciplines of weekly worship, daily prayer, daily scripture reading, weekly cell group participation, regular theological conversation, hands-on mission involvement, intentional listening, and high stewardship. Board members hold one another accountable for the "spiritual life" just as they hold one another accountable to the policies of the church.

Lead the Sacrifice

Each member of the visionary board is expected to apply the same intentionality to measure the cost of discipleship on their own lives, as the entire board does for the organization. Personal risk management follows the same pattern as corporate risk management. Board members consider what they personally must put at stake for the mission and vision to succeed:

- *Heritage:* What personal, marriage, or family habits must change to align oneself with the vision and mission?
- *Attitude:* What biases, prejudices, or assumptions must be adjusted to align oneself with the vision and mission?
- *Lifestyle:* What personal priorities, perks, or privileges must be surrendered; and what priorities, obligations, or responsibilities need to be added to align oneself with the vision and mission?
- *Personnel:* What changes in official status, authority, or deployment of energy must take place to align oneself with the vision and mission?
- *Organization:* What roles, responsibilities, or agendas must be shifted to align oneself with the vision and mission?
- *Property:* What changes in personal accommodation, office space, or communication methods must be changed to align oneself with the vision and mission?
- *Finance:* What changes in remuneration, expense accounts, or personal investments must be changed to align oneself with the vision and mission?

Board members are twice as diligent to define their personal "cost of discipleship," and twice as scrupulous to "pay the price" for the vision and mission to succeed. Leaders lead the sacrifice so that the rest of the organization can follow.

A common question about the leadership of sacrifice reveals the fundamental issue of leadership. People ask: "Do you mean alignment with organizational vision and mission, or with personal vision and mission?" The very question reveals the difference between traditional, modern boards and servant-empowering, visionary boards. Traditional boards allow an acceptable difference between organizational and personal mission. In servant-empowering organizations boards require a direct and consistent alignment between organizational and personal mission. When organizational and personal mission are separated, board members can only lead *by authority.* When organizational and personal mission are aligned, board members lead *by credibility.*

Criteria for Visionary Board Membership

It should be obvious by now that the criteria for visionary board membership in a servant-empowering organization is different from that of traditional organizations. These are leaders who understand that they will influence the organization more by their credibility than by their authority. They are prepared to align personal mission and organizational mission, and they will use language such as "ownership," "surrender," and "passion" to describe their dedication to merge lifestyle with work.

Traditional board members are often chosen because they bring either seniority or expertise to the organization. They are members of the board because their families have been on the board for generations, and they are the most senior members of the church. Or, they are members of the board because they have professional expertise (legal, educational, administrative, financial, or theological) that contributes to task management. Both criteria are useless to the visionary board. Seniority is often more preoccupied with self-interest than with building genuine consensus of spirituality. Expertise is important, but only in the context of teams and team coordination, and not for visioning the future.

Ability to Focus the Future

First, board members for a servant-empowering organization are chosen because they can *focus the future*. Therefore, they have abilities to read demographic trends, observe the pace of change, and converse with community leaders. They have the abilities to ponder sacred texts, reflect on spirit and culture, and pray.

Their instincts are able to predict where positive and negative relevance will occur fifteen years down the road, and their courage is able to establish the price the organization must pay to face the future and grow. They ensure the high impact of the organization on the surrounding cultures.

Ability to Mentor the Membership

Second, board members for a servant-empowering organization are chosen because they can *mentor the membership*. Therefore, they have inclinations to model the spirituality of the organization, guide others to align their lives with that vision and mission, and coach others into lives of self-discipline and sacrifice for the sake of the vision and mission. In short, they can mentor individuals to mature as organizational members, emerge as team leaders, and perhaps become future board members. They protect the longevity and integrity of the organization.

Board membership is a very high standard of spiritual leadership. This is why in many organizations the president or pastor may handpick board members, or, if they are nominated and elected, the president or pastor will be highly influential in the process.

Measuring Success

How does a board measure success? At the end of the year, as they look back over the seeming chaos of activities initiated, completed, or in process, how do board members judge whether the organization has been both faithful and fruitful?

Statistics are often only moderately helpful, and sometimes misleading. Churches, for example, often measure membership, deficits or surpluses, or the increase or decrease of conflict, which reveal very little about success. They may measure worship attendance, team multiplication, or the increase or decrease of creative ideas, which are more helpful, and yet which *by themselves* do not assure a visionary board of success. Fundamentally, the board needs to know if they have remained faithful to who they are, and if anticipated changes have happened. In church terminology, the board needs to know where Jesus was amid the many microcultures, and if the church did everything possible to join Jesus there.

The following are the key questions asked by a servant-empowering board:

Focus the Future

The board needs to know if the trajectory of mission is aligned or sidetracked, and if it is intersecting the microcultures of the mission market or marginalizing people.

- Is the world any different?
- Has the positive relevance of the organization increased?
- Has the potential for negative relevance been avoided?
- Has the organization achieved anticipated results in personal and social change?

If not, it is up to the board to discover why and initiate whatever changes in heritage, attitude, lifestyle, personnel, office, property, and finance are necessary to turn it around. If so, it is up to the board to increase their ambitions and add new trajectories of mission that will intersect new microcultures in new ways.

Mentor the Membership

The board needs to know if the organizational membership is maturing, and if new team leaders are emerging who can impact the mission market in innovative ways.

- Are more leaders emerging?
- Is the spirituality embedded?
- Is the spiritual discipline serious?
- Are members paying the necessary price for success?

If not, it is up to the board to invest more time to model and mentor organizational members, and to lead the way in sacrificial surrender to vision and mission. If so, it is up to the board to expand their mentoring role to the edges and margins of organizational life.

Conclusion

We return to the metaphor of waves sculpting the landscape of mission. Visionary boards ride the crest of the wave. In other words, they are not *in* the chaos of teams spraying the shoreline with creative, missional energy, but they *surf the chaos.* They have the *vision* to see over the breakers and beyond the horizon, the *balance* to intuitively do what is faithful, the *instinct* to make the right choices and tough decisions, and the *serenity* to manage risk.

Empowering Management

Visionary boards delegate management authority to a trusted, gifted few. Two things are crucial for the servant-empowering organization. First, the visionary board delegates real power, not just the appearance of power. The board is not going to look over their shoulders, second-guess strategies, or delay implementation so that they can give a particular tactic more study. Second, the management with which the gifted few are entrusted is proscriptive management. Visionary boards are not empowering management to control organizational teams and tactics, but to guard boundaries, encourage and equip creativity, and protect safety. This is a different kind of management.

I most often refer to this style of management as "stability in chaos." A management team brings stability (i.e., safety, quality, and coordination) into what is otherwise a chaos of team initiative. Without this kind of management, the plethora of multiplying teams would quickly fragment the organization and undermine mission impact. They would get in one another's way, compete for resources, and eventually dissipate energy in fruitless adventures. Management in a servant-empowering organizations transforms Don Quixote into Thomas Edison, Nelson Mandela, or Winston Churchill.

Management's Function

If we return to the metaphor of the wave, we see that servant-empowering management occurs in the hidden depths of wave formation. It is never particularly visible in organizational life, from inside or outside. Indeed, if it is visible to the insider or the newcomer, it is probably not doing its job properly. No glory adheres in management–and management should have no glory. It's a difficult, mundane, and very necessary job that deserves and receives no publicity. Management is what happens in the depths of the sea that is crucial to the formation of waves. Management helps create the curve, intensity, and direction of each wave or true team, and aligns each wave or team to follow relentlessly the same course, so that the shoreline or mission market is sculpted and transformed in accord with the goals or ends policies of the organization.

Management in a servant-empowering organization functions very differently from management in a traditional modern organization. The offices and titles may sound the same (CEO, COO, etc.), but what these people do is very different. In the traditional modern organization, management is the taskmaster. They initiate action, recruit implementation, approve planning, supervise action, and reserve the right to evaluate success. Managers are in control. In the servant-empowering organization, management is the boundary-keeper. They grow leaders, equip teams, align mission, and stay out of the way. Traditional management manages programs; servant-empowering management manages leaders. It is as simple and complex as that.

The Team Leader and Management

The real control of program is entrusted to team leaders and true teams. They have the power to discern, design, implement, and evaluate mission, and they do not have to get permission from management. Management asks four questions of every creative idea:

- Does it emerge from the personal and spiritual growth of the team leader or true team?
- Is it within the boundaries of organizational core values and beliefs?
- Is it aligned with overall organizational vision and mission?
- If all that is true, how can management equip the team to be as successful as they can possibly be?

Helping the team become a success at whatever it is called to do is the whole purpose of management. It does not matter if management personalities agree with the team's purpose or tactics. It does not matter if the team creativity offends their aesthetic tastes, personal ideologies, individual theological perspectives, or sense of propriety and tradition. These are irrelevant. What matters is that the team mission evolves from personal and spiritual growth, is within the boundaries, is aligned with the target, and is magnificently successful. Therefore:

- management is constantly fueling personal and spiritual growth so that creative ideas will be elicited from the imaginations of growing staff and volunteers;
- management is constantly refining and embedding core values and beliefs into the habits of organizational life;
- management is constantly aligning and targeting team mission to the larger organizational vision and mission;
- and management is constantly equipping and training teams to be as efficient and effective, and as liberated and unobtrusive, as possible.

Management Methods

Management can do all this any way they want. They can use any tactic, partner with any consultant or agency, or use any resource and develop any budget they wish. The visionary board doesn't really care how it gets done. However, the board does limit management options. The board insists that management stay within boundaries of core values, beliefs, vision, and mission; and that management models and embeds certain processes or habits of decision-making; and that management avoids doing certain things that might jeopardize the safety, or undermine the growth, or inhibit the initiative of all of the true teams. As long as management stays within the ends policies, process policies, and selected executive limitations of the board, they can do whatever they want instantly and immediately without the express permission of the board and without the burden of constant progress reports. Just do it.

The Contrast to Traditional Management

The more one describes empowering management, the more the contrast with traditional modern management emerges, and the more the stress level of traditional organizational leaders and members rises.

A TRUSTED, GIFTED FEW

First, the board delegates management to a trusted, gifted few. Take particular note of the wording of that statement.

- *The board must reasonably trust management.*
  This is not blind trust. It is reasonable trust because the board refines the "spirituality" of the organization and expects management to model their behavior. They define key ends policies and procedural habits, and strategic executive limitations. Reasonable trust means that the boundaries for action are so clear that management can be held accountable, not only by the board, but by even the least important member of the organization, and by even the most remote observer from outside culture. Reasonable trust implies absolute transparency. Duplicitous management cannot hide behind innumerable by-laws or remain camouflaged in the midst of ambiguous mission statements. On the other hand, high integrity management does not need to fear the interference of intimidating personalities or being overruled by meddling self-interests.

- *The managers must be "gifted."*
  The same characteristics of a team leader apply to them also. They must be passionate, called, competent, accountable, and spiritual. The same evaluative criteria applied to team leaders apply them also. They must be aligned to the mission of the organization, able to

model high integrity, compulsive about continuous learning, and able to work as a team. It is no longer possible to be a great manager for a widget company, and then change jobs to become a great manager of a wicket company, as if the product doesn't matter. The product is all that matters, and great managers know it. They have to *love* the product–and be prepared to surrender life and lifestyle for mission results.

- *This is management by "the few" rather than "the many."*
Empowering organizations do not need many managers, because managers are not supervising innumerable tasks but guiding a larger synergy of personal growth, innovation, and productivity. Large bureaucracies are unnecessary because managers create the conditions of reasonable trust for teams and let them go. Neither is there any threat that managers will become dictators, because management does not "dictate" any particular tactics. It guards boundaries, grows leaders, and allows teams to innovate. If anything, the function of good management is to "dictate" that no one can "dictate." It is to create the high trust, motivated environment for creative, productive chaos to happen.

It is not difficult to understand the stress that many modern traditional managers feel if their organization is transitioning to servant empowerment. They have lived all their lives hidden in a large, slow-moving, redundant bureaucracy in which unpleasant jobs can easily be avoided and in which unexpected failures can easily be blamed on someone else. The reduction (and indeed the elimination) of chaos is the primary goal of traditional management, even at the risk of stifling creativity. Suddenly the servant-empowering organization insists that managers be passionate, called, competent, accountable, and spiritual; that managers focus on results rather than process; and that management become transparently accountable to everyone within and beyond the organization. Such stress can lead to the wholesale firing, early retirement, or resignation of former managers. Who will replace them? A new breed of manager will. These leaders have never fit into the large bureaucracy, but can now come into their own.

Manage Leadership Development

Second, empowering management does not manage program development. They manage leadership development. This is not to say that the servant-empowering organization will have no "programs." Indeed, the servant-empowering organization will have many programs, strategies, initiatives, resources that will grow and thrive, peak and perish, replace other programs and be replaced by other programs. They will be as many, and as powerful, as the droplets of water that spray the beach and sculpt the cultural landscape. Yet "management" will not control that. Teams control that; and team leaders are the key to the power of teams. Empowering management pays relatively little attention to programs. They invest all their energy in multiplying team leaders.

- Empowering management makes sure that leaders are constantly emerging with focused mission attitudes, rigorous work ethics, pragmatic adaptability, relentless persistence, and high self-esteem. If they can continually grow these leaders, then the leaders will innovate the programs, and the organization will achieve mission results.
- Empowering management helps resource the team leader to shape a team that is passionate, called, competent, accountable, and spiritual. Managers become the primary resource of the team leader, not to command the tactics that the team must obey, but to equip the team to develop the best tactics.

This is not to say that there will be no management budget. It means there will be a budget-of-budgets. There will be an operating budget for management that provides resources that all teams share and a capital pool for investment that will encourage every team to develop its own budget. Management does not subsidize programs. It subsidizes leaders. The best way to subsidize programs is to pay for it all through a unified budget. The best way to subsidize leaders is to seed their initiatives through capital pools. Transfer power to raise and administer funds to the same people who are motivated and equipped to use it.

LETTING GO OF CONTROL

The final stress is the discovery that the power of management no longer lies in control, but in strategically letting go of control. It is not in supervision, but in training. It is not in tasks, but in boundaries. It is not in unified budgets, but in seed money. It is not in giving or withholding permission, but in constant motivation and education. If the management by a trusted, gifted few raises the stress level of traditional modern managers, then letting go of control raises the stress level of traditional modern organizational members. Most traditional organizational members and employees (whether in the church, nonprofit agency, or corporate environment) do not want to be empowered. They prefer to be controlled. It is more comfortable to be told what to do than to be expected to take responsibility for results. It is easier to grumble about management from the relative ease of disempowerment, than it is to accept real power and be expected to succeed. Letting go of control means higher expectations for attitude, integrity, competency, and teamwork. Some volunteers and employees currently in committees or employed in tasks will drop out. They will be replaced by leaders who have always chafed under authority, but who thrive under the pressure of creative responsibility.

Management Configuration

The configuration of the management team follows the process of leadership development, rather than the need to oversee program development.

Deployed at Crucial Turning Points of Leadership Development

In other words, rather than deploy managers to look after a particular "silo" of programs and a particular section of a unified budget, the servant-empowering organization deploys managers at the crucial turning points of leadership development. These are the places in organizational life that are most fragile, delicate, and decisive for organizational growth and eventual mission success. For example, the core discipling process of a church is that every day, in every way, every member of the church is in process of being changed, gifted, called, equipped, and sent.

- Lives are *changed* and transformed through worship and the touch of the Holy.
- People are discovering their unique *gifts* that they can contribute to God's mission on earth.
- Christians discern their *calling* as a personal mission that will shape vocation and lifestyle.
- Disciples are *equipped* with whatever skills are necessary to accomplish what they are called to do.
- Servants are *sent* to accomplish their called mission with the highest degree of excellence.

Empowering church organizations, therefore, do not deploy managers to work *within* each of the stages of development. The programs and budgets *within* each stage of development are best managed by teams relevant to the task. Instead, the church deploys managers *in between* these stages. These transition points are the most vulnerable points in the leadership development process. The crucial moments in leadership development are the points between life change and discovery of gifts; or between celebration of gifts and discernment of call; or between discernment of call and quality training; or between quality training and courage to act; or between action and even more life change. These points are where the risk is greatest. That is where leaders need guidance. That is where empowering church organizations deploy managers.

In the past, I have usually described the management team as a "stability triangle" in order to emphasize its *function* to bring stability and direction into the barely contained chaos of team multiplication. However, I have learned that it is equally important to describe the configuration of management staff in a way that reflects their *intervention* to maintain the synergy of leadership development. It is more important to understand management as a means to strategically intervene in organizational life to keep the momentum of leadership development going. (Note: We will see this diagram adapted again in the next section about leadership development, as the organization develops senior staff to mirror the management that maintains synergy for leadership development.)

Maintaining Synergy

I have adapted the diagram above to reflect the example of church development. The management team does not maintain programming, but rather synergy for leadership development. Their job is not to ensure the survival or even the effectiveness of worship, Sunday school, fellowship groups, counseling practices, and so on; their job is to ensure the growth and effectiveness of leaders. These leaders will develop teams, and these teams will have complete freedom to develop the tactics that get mission results that are timely and relevant. Management has no vested interest in tactics, or in one tactic over another, or in the survival of any particular tactic. Their vested interest is the development of leaders who can innovate maximum mission results as defined by the board.

Five Necessary Managers

Therefore, management is configured to follow the leadership development process. Theoretically, the church (and any organization) can be run by five people. Even if the church (or any organization) is very small, management still consists of five basic interventions that keep the synergy of leadership development going.

- *Motivation:* Management equips teams to excite an attitude for personal growth. In a church, one of the most basic functions of the Sunday morning experience (worship services and hospitality) is to draw seekers and disciples into a constant discipline of personal and spiritual growth. Yes, there is a sense in which worship itself provides content for personal and spiritual growth, but leadership development will not happen in a single hour on a single morning. Worship is a spark for a larger process of discovery, discernment, and outreach. Various team leaders and teams develop the programs for worship, but the servant-empowering manager intervenes to align the mission, support high integrity, facilitate training, and build team spirit.

  The management intervention for "motivation" is often overlooked among nonprofit (and corporate) organizations. The tactic may not be a Sunday morning experience of hospitality and worship, but an organization must have an intentional vehicle to motivate volunteers and employees to celebrate corporate spirit, and encourage self-sacrifice to achieve a higher goal. The more self-centered and individualistic Western culture has become, the more this management role becomes a full-time job.

- *Personal Development:* Management equips teams to provide multiple options for personal growth. These options vary by content and learning methodology, and they touch all aspects of personal growth (intellectual, emotional, relational, and so on). The servant-empowering manager does not develop and maintain the programs, however. The servant-empowering manager strategically intervenes to help team leaders mature both seekers and disciples.

  The management intervention for personal development is too often limited to professional training, and the learning methodology is too often focused on practicing techniques. Mentoring is the most fundamental tool for personal development. This may be the mutual mentoring of small groups or the one-to-one mentoring between "guide" and "apprentice." It shapes not only the action, but the entire lifestyle and life cycle of the volunteer or employee, seamlessly uniting personal growth and professional practice.

- *Missionary Deployment:* Management equips teams to target the mission market and deliver hope to every microculture efficiently and effectively. Certainly the experience of grace transcends ultimate human control, and the confidence of salvation is beyond human guarantees, but the organizational aim is to proclaim "good news," model reconciliation, provide the means for others to share abundant life. The success of that mission, in any given microculture, demands acute sensitivities and complicated skills.

  The management intervention for missionary deployment is, as always, focused on leadership development rather than program development. It is not for management to package resources, but it is their task to mentor, equip, and launch leaders. Leadership development is not complete until gifted, called, and equipped organizational members are actually engaged *beyond the organization* in the mission market.

- *Training:* Management equips teams...to equip teams...that equip teams. Training pervades every aspect of the organization, but a distinct management intervention embeds the habit of training throughout the system. The single most common vulnerability in organizational efficiency is that training breaks down. Either the organization succeeds and begins assimilating or deploying leaders with undue haste, or the organization fails and allows leaders to remain active without constant upgrades. Either way, a key management role is to intervene to accelerate the training habit.

  Management embeds the training habit through combinations of basic training and ongoing upgrades "on-the-job," and through internal training and outsourced training with other agencies. The demand for training opportunities relevant to the fragmenting diversity of the mission market is so great that servant-empowering organizations broker continuing education partnerships in innumerable directions.

- *Operations:* Management equips teams by providing resources that benefit everyone. Property and technology is accessible to all teams. An operational budget provides communication systems available for all. Money is set aside to "seed" program development emerging from individual teams. Servant-empowering management monitors acceptable standards of accounting to protect the corporate status of the organization.

  Most churches, and many other organizations, reduce "management" to "operations"–and thereby deprive managers of anything of real substance to "operate." Management ends up manipulating budgets and resources with no reference to their purpose and intent. "Operations" only makes sense if there is a leadership development process to "operate."

Note that I have described these five positions as "interventions" rather than just "functions." The key to servant-empowering management is not that they develop programs that *do* these stages, but that they intervene to move people from one stage to another. Individual teams will *do* various tactics for each of these stages; where they need help is in passing people along from one stage to another.

Together the five management interventions grow the leaders who will get mission results. They work in alignment with the ends policies of the board, practicing the procedural habits prescribed by the board, and avoiding executive limitations proscribed by the board. In a sense, each of the five management pieces is a "capital pool." Each management position can spend their "capital pool" in any way the manager thinks to be efficient and effective in achieving their goal in the leadership development process. The capital pool for "operations" is just one "capital pool" among five, although a treasurer or financial officer can hold money for the use of each pool.

Management does not primarily interface with a board. They develop budgets, spend money from capital pools, innovate ways to grow leaders, and intervene to move volunteers and employees *between* functions and program silos. They do all this without having to consult with, or report to, the board. Management consists of a trusted, gifted few. The separation of board and management is important. The more they connect with each other, the more likely board members will become sidetracked by management decisions and managers will become sidetracked by policy development decisions. Organizational visioning will be weakened on the one hand; and leadership development will slow down on the other hand.

Management/Team Interface

Management must interface with all of the different teams. At any given time, in any given crisis or transition, management and team will intersect in one of five ways. The diagram below may be in black-and-white, but imagine each molecule below in a different color to represent the enormous variety of teams. The central molecule is "green" to signify the nurturing role of "management."

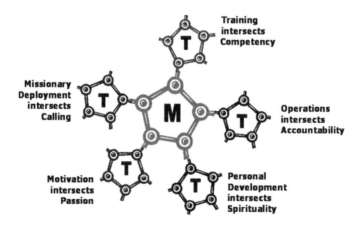

Each team intersects with management at different times, in different circumstances, with different aspects of team and management life. The intersection can be initiated by either party. Teams will be primarily motivated by crisis, and management will be primarily motivated by habit. In other words, it is the anticipated habit of management to deliberately connect with teams regarding motivation, personal development, missionary deployment, training, and operations. And it is the emerging crisis or unexpected challenge to passion, spirituality, calling, competency, and accountability that drives teams to connect with management.

It is not difficult to imagine intricate patterns of interconnection developing in organizational life. Note, however, that intersection with the board is not the primary image. The board is not involved in team life. The board is on the "crest of the wave" and not among the "spray" of droplets on the landscape. Management, however, lies in the depth of the wave and is intimately connected with the "spray" on the landscape. Management guides the direction, intensity, and impact of the mission.

Two Fundamental Currents

The "connectivity" of management and teams implies that a servant-empowering organization has two fundamental currents to the practice of management. Using the metaphor of the "wave," I describe these two fundamental currents as "impact" and "undertow." Every wave involves both the force of the wave that impacts the beach and the suction of the wave as it recedes from the beach. Hidden in the depths of the wave, management observes the "spray" as true teams sculpt the cultural landscape and measures two things to guide their habit of "connectivity" with teams.

IMPACT AND RISK MANAGEMENT

The "impact" of the wave requires risk management. Managers constantly measure the cost of innovation against the cost of failure. The higher the risk, the more urgent it is for management to connect with the team in the appropriate ways (i.e., for motivation, personal growth, missionary deployment, training, and/or operations). High risk does *not* mean abandonment of innovation, just as high innovation does *not* mean bracing for likely failure.

High risk means that management must strategically intervene to ensure success or learn from failure. Risk management is not a method to determine whether to give or withhold permission to do something. Servant-empowering managers are not in the business of checking innovation or holding back experimentation.

Risk management is a method to anticipate constantly how teams will need to be equipped and how teams will need to learn. Risk management is a constant process of refinement and adjustment. If the ocean fails to erode the seashore, that does not mean the ocean stops producing waves. It means that the wave motion will be refined and adjusted until, eventually, the sea is victorious. It is the same with servant-empowering management. Managers measure risk to achieve results.

UNDERTOW REQUIRES GRIEVANCE PROCESS

The "undertow" of the wave requires a grievance process. Managers must maintain a "feedback" loop that helps them identify problems in leadership development. This is not a vehicle for program complaints. Management does not do program development. Program complaints should go directly to the teams that are responsible for programs. However, management is about leadership development, and if staff or volunteers are intentionally or unintentionally subverting organizational mission, contradicting organizational values and convictions, or transgressing executive limitations, then management needs to know and act. A good grievance process will be transparent, accessible, and clear enough to help management differentiate between immature blunders and human rights violations. It should warn the organization about public relations nightmares or potential litigation. Just as the "undertow" draws the sand and silt that are the products of erosion back into the sea, so also the grievance process draws the by-products of mission back into the organization for examination. If leaders are going astray, managers in charge of leadership development need to know.

Conclusion

Servant-empowering organizations allow for a much greater complexity in organizational life than traditional modern leaders might imagine. The old organizational model foresees one board, one management team, and multiple task groups. The servant-empowering organizational model foresees the possibility of one board, a multiple nexus of management, and multiplying self-sustaining teams. It is not difficult to apply the principles of management described above to the function of any complex team or to the partnership of a cluster of teams. Team leaders in more complex projects will find themselves developing leaders in exactly the same fashion attributed here to a "management team." The diagram to "maintain synergy" could be simply a close-up snap-shot of just one area of an organizational organism with many tentacles.

Servant-empowering organizations can thus be adaptive and effective in the fast-paced world of change precisely because they deploy management to manage leadership development rather than program silos. Management is not fixed, but flowing. They are not locked into budget lines, are not immersed in progress reports, and will not bog down in turf protection. Their concern is leadership development. They mentor and equip. They intervene at the right place, at the right time, with the right team leader…and at all other times they get out of the way.

The Dynamic of Spirited Leadership

Team Oversight

The Power of More

The Dynamic of
Spirited Leadership

A Servant-empowering organization requires a "spirited" leader. This is the leader who keeps "first things first" in the life of the organization. He or she demonstrates and mentors unconditional loyalty to the higher purpose of the organization, and ultimate concern for the cause or the "heartburst" public addressed by the organization. She or he articulates and defends the sacred boundaries of the organization. The leader reveals and maintains the credible authority of leadership. The leader is "charismatic" in the ancient sense of that word. The leader is filled with the "spirit" of the organization. Look into the leader's eyes, watch the leader's behavior, listen to the leader's words, and observe the leader's sacrifices, and you will see the essence of the organization itself.

Defining Leadership

Although I once used the term "servant leadership" because it seemed so parallel to the term "servant-empowering organization," I do so no longer. The term "servant leadership" is too confusing. It has been used to justify task management as well as policy governance, mere equipping as well as long-range visioning, and control maintenance as well as innovation. It begs three questions:

1. Servant of whom?

The only viable answer is that they are servants of "God." This might seem obviously true for churches and less obviously true for nonprofit or for-profit organizations, but "God" is whatever power makes an absolute claim upon the unconditional loyalty and ultimate concern of the organization. It is that which is "wholly other" than the mere self-interest of the individual leaders or members, and which is "wholly dedicated" to the well being of the world.

Defined this way, the great irony of our time is that many nonprofit and even for-profit leaders are more clearly servants of "God" than church leaders. Church leaders are too often servants of ideology, dogma, polity, tradition, or ego. When it comes to the bottom line, church leaders are less prepared to make ultimate sacrifices for absolute claims than many social service and health care workers, and many corporate CEOs and presidents.

The leader is definitely *not* a servant of the organization. He or she is not subject to directives from a task management board, nor from a denominational hierarchy. Leaders are servants of a "higher power" that makes an "absolute claim" upon both leader and organization, whose "claim" is the whole reason the organization exists in the first place. This is why the Spirited Leader can hold the organization accountable to alignment with the vision and mission. He or she is "filled with the Spirit."

2. Trainer of what?

The answer is more complex than is usually supposed. Spirited Leaders train the four basic parts of accountability: mission attitude, high integrity, skills competency, and teamwork. They do not just equip skills or impart knowledge. They hire, train, evaluate, and fire on the basis of these four keys to accountability. Their authority is greater than that of a servant. It is more akin to the authority of the ancient martial arts master to a disciple.

Spirited Leaders are mentors who work first and foremost with their immediate small group of disciples.

- They mentor the alignment of both professional and private life with the vision and mission of the organization, so that organizational service is a seamless 24/7 experience. They clarify the vision and focus the mission. They keep the disciples from being sidetracked by self-concerned or subtle manipulations.
- They equip specific skills, or, better stated, they equip the ability to develop and pursue a continuing education path. They cannot equip every skill, or even outsource every program need in this rapidly changing mission environment. They can and must train disciples to customize their own path to enlightened competency.
- They coach the disciples in the art of teamwork. This is more a matter of "good timing" than "strategic planning." It is the art of knowing when to be patient and when to be challenging; when to speak and when to be silent; when to intervene and when to let teammates do it themselves. It is the art of cooperation.

Spirited Leaders are definitely *not* omni-competent in all the abilities required by a growing organization. The leaders may not even be particularly good at some of the classic tasks of administration or program development. They are excellent, however, in their ability to hold disciples to the accountability of mission, integrity, constant learning, and teamwork.

3. Leader to where?

The answer is both mystical and practical, and again it is surprising that nonprofit and for-profit CEO's often see this more clearly than the average church pastor. The Spirited Leader leads wherever the Spirit directs! The only way to intuit where the Spirit is going is to immerse oneself in the spirituality of the organization and the reality of the mission market.

Spirited Leaders, like servant-empowering boards, draw a line between purpose and conviction, and then extend it over time and space through all the multiple subcultures that surround the organization. They look for the points of intersection, either as opportunities or obstacles, and position the organization to seize the one and avoid the other. It is simple in concept, but difficult in practice. That's why Spirited Leaders work with visionary boards.

The Spirited Leader is definitely *not* leading the organization toward maintenance, preservation, or survival. He or she is leading the organization ever deeper into the mission market. The leader's intention is to reshape the cultural landscape. If leaders are merciless with organizational members, it is not because they do not care about the members, but because they care far more about the mission. They are *urgent*.

Conclusion

"Spirited Leadership" is a clearer term than "Servant Leadership" because it underlines the *authority* of leadership without assuming *hierarchy* in leadership. Hierarchical leadership (both by office and consensus management) maintains the *solidity* of an organization. They want the organization to be predictable, manageable, controllable, stable, and calm. Unfortunately, a calm sea never reshapes the cultural landscape. Spirited leadership maintains the *fluidity* of an organization. They want the organization to be creative, empowering, innovative, volatile, and turgid. They send waves of teams to impact the beach and carve the cultural landscape.

I have deliberately been ambiguous referring to "Spirited Leadership" in the singular and the plural. This is because the servant-empowering organization does not require a single leader to be intimately involved in everything. Indeed, this is precisely the kind of leadership the servant-empowering organization resists. As soon as an organization relies on one, or a small handful, of leaders to competently lead every task, the mission is held hostage by the slowest learner and the most mediocre performer. Even if they have noble visions, these slow movers will eventually freeze solid in a hostile environment. The servant empowered organization will have both a single Spirited Leader and a team of Spirited Leaders ...and, as the organization grows, it may be difficult to separate master mentor from mentoring disciples.

Team Oversight

One way to picture the behavior of Spirited Leaders is to describe the template of how teams meet. Teams are the fundamental mission unit of the servant-empowering organization, and even the most complex organizations function in the same template. They are simply larger, more complicated aggregates of true teams. Similarly, team leaders are a micro-version of the Spirited Leader of the entire organization. The Spirited Leader works with a small group of leaders, who in turn work with a small group of leaders, who in turn work with a small group of leaders, ad infinitum. The Spirited Leader of a large organization grew from being the Spirited Leader of a small team—and kept applying the same principles.

The Preparation for Team Meeting

Spirited Leaders are insistent that teams meet. There are no excuses other than health, and even that can often be overcome by long-distance participation. Because the mission is *urgent,* team members cannot suddenly decide to take a day off, dally in the coffee room, or catch up on e-mail. However, Spirited Leaders will recognize that if the team members are being successfully mentored, and are truly aligned to mission, they will *also be urgent* to get on with their work.

Each team will customize its own covenant around frequency, length of time, location, and technology of meeting. Spirited Leaders know it is crucial to clarify that team meetings never happen unless team members do their "homework" first. Never come to a meeting unprepared. Never come to a meeting merely to report. And never, ever come to a meeting expecting to get help in planning and implementation, or to get permission to do a task.

The "homework" of a team member is the preparation they need to do to participate in the agenda of the meeting. Of course, this means the team member (who is a "spirited leader" for his or her own team) must review the status of the work. He or she must bring to the meeting a background awareness of the projects, mission market expectations, leadership training and deployment, and financial and other resources necessary for their particular sphere of influence. However, this background awareness is *not* the content that will be shared in the meeting. Instead, this awareness helps the team member list in advance the following key issues that *will* be brought to the meeting:

- *Alignment questions:* The team member identifies any areas of work that are questionably aligned with the vision, mission, values, and beliefs of the larger organization, and is prepared to seek guidance from the Spirited Leader to laser-target tasks, leaders, resources, etc., in his or her sphere of influence to the mission of the organization.
- *Training needs:* The team member lists any particular areas of training *beyond that which he or she already accomplished with his or her team,* and for which he or she requires guidance to find or obtain the necessary training. The Spirited Leader helps the member customize a learning path.
- *Resource needs:* The team member lists any particular financial gaps or communication needs *beyond that which is already budgeted or provided in the organization,* which must be addressed through the larger management of the organization. The Spirited Leader connects the member to find or develop new resources.
- *Work convergences:* The team member lists the places in any given project that impinge upon or overlap the work of other team members in their sphere of influence, flagging areas of collaboration that will be relevantly addressed between those leaders *outside the team meeting.* The Spirited Leader has little to do with this, and assumes team members will take initiative.
- *Irresolvable problems:* The team member lists any challenge or issue that he or she could not resolve, so that the entire team can troubleshoot what appears to be an irresolvable problem. The Spirited Leader contributes to a larger conversation that brainstorms fresh ideas to seize unexpected opportunities or overcome unexpected obstacles.

This is the "homework" that Spirited Leaders expect every team member will bring to the team. Every member in *this* team will be a *leader* of a second team. One team should never duplicate or even review the work that is done by the other team. If a member of a team brings "homework" from another team in which he or she is supposedly the leader, the Spirited Leader will question his or her competence or addictive need to control.

The Team Meeting

Once the team actually meets, the template for their agenda is constant. They may spend more or less time on various items of the template, but the basics remain the same. The agenda is basically divided into three parts: mission focus time, leadership development time, and problem-solving time.

1. Mission Focus Time

I have shared elsewhere the keywords for reviewing the effectiveness and efficiency of core values, beliefs, vision, and mission in the organization. This is a process of "RAETT-ing" the mission of the team.

Refine: Core values, beliefs, vision, and mission must be tested against the complexity and constant change of the organization. Every team member must continuously study the "margins." Who is left out of their sphere of influence?

Align: Projects must be designed, and leaders deployed, for clear mission goals and nothing else. Every team member must continuously study the "sidetracks." Where are we wasting energy?

Embed: Core values, beliefs, vision, and mission must be revealed in our actual work and the lifestyles of team members. Every team member must continuously study the "failures." Where did we fall short?

Team: Work must be done in high trust, mutual support, and constant communication within the team. Every team member must continuously study the "burnouts." Who is overwhelmed?

Target: Teams must focus on those partners and projects that can become "living proof" of the larger organizational values, beliefs, vision, and mission. Team members must continuously study the "irrelevancies." Who is indifferent to our existence?

In the context of a team meeting, the Spirited Leader invites every team member to highlight any concerns about their leadership in their own sphere of influence, or that of any other member of the team as they lead in their sphere of influence.

This exercise can even be quantified. Each team member can "RAETT" their colleagues on a scale of 1–10 with "10" being a perfect score. This could become more or less detailed. Team members could be asked to share their own "RAETT-ing" of every project in their sphere of influence, or "RAETT-ing" for the structure, financial management, training, resource development, and communications in their sphere of influence.

- Anything or anyone scoring between "8" and "9" deserves special mentoring from the team leader for mission attitude and integrity.
- Anything or anyone scoring between "5" and "8" requires special intervention for training in skills and team cooperation.
- Anything or anyone scoring between less than "5" should be considered for termination or dismissal.

The Spirited Leader will not cover all five aspects of focused mission in every meeting. The "homework" of the team members will reveal where the mentoring must focus at any given time.

Spirited Leaders understand that failure to get mission results is not primarily due to performance. Traditional organizational meetings waste leadership energy reviewing tasks and training skills. The former should have been done by team members before coming to the meeting, and the latter can be outsourced as needed. Mission failure happens because leaders are too narrow-minded, diverted by relative trivialities, overcome by guilt or personal neediness, overly controlling, or indifferent to opportunities and obstacles. Whether or not the Spirited Leader use a tool of "RAETT-ing" in this way, they must address the fundamental causes for mission failure. They cannot allow themselves to be drawn into the management of any particular area of work, because mere management will never maximize mission impact.

2. Leadership Development Time

Spirited Leaders engage the team with an assessment of their current leadership development, and focus on one or more aspects of growth. Training actually consists of four areas of encouragement:

1. *Mission Attitude:* Every team member or leader needs to constantly focus his or her mission attitude in the midst of changing circumstances in personal life, mission engagement, and congregational growth.
2. *High Integrity:* Every team member or leader needs to be constantly challenged to model the core values and beliefs of the organization in both professional and personal lives.
3. *Skills Development:* Every team member or leader needs to identify areas of weakness and develop a learning strategy to improve whatever skills are emerging as necessary to get mission results.
4. *Teamwork:* Every team member or leader needs to hone his or her ability to personally and prayerfully support, cooperate with, and communicate with the other members of the team.

Spirited Leaders will address one or more of these challenges with the team. Their expectation is that each team member will take the learning back to his or her own secondary team meeting in which he or she is the spirited leader.

Just as task group meetings in traditional organizations waste time on reporting and program development, so also they waste time on conflict resolution. Spirited Leaders understand that control, not conflict, is the root cause of bad leadership. Therefore, their goal is not to resolve conflict, but to break control. Control occurs when the foundation of trust has become unclear. Team members become egotistical to garner praise, or fearful of mistakes, or jealous of success, or disrespectful of the creativity of others. Rigorous accountability in these four areas helps team members restore reasonable trust. Once obsessive and hidden needs to control are broken, most conflict disappears.

3. Problem-solving Time

The Spirited Leader matches the emerging crises of team members with the opportunities and obstacles that result from the intersections of organizational mission with changing cultures. He or she leads the team to address any crisis or challenge that could not be resolved by the team member with his or her own team. It may involve any number of implementation issues regarding program, resource, volunteers, finances, and so on.

Spirited Leaders identify "convergences" of passion, calling, networks, or programs. Much "problem solving" is really a matter of identifying "convergences" between the work of one team member and the work of another team member. Problems tend to go away when team members are consulting with one another "on-the-fly," on a daily basis, through various technologies used to discuss priorities and allocations of resources.

A "hierarchy" of interventions emerges in the life of any team, ranging from the most general to the most specific. These are well identified by Patrick Lencioni.[1]

- The most common failing of a team is lack of trust, or, the inability to embed the core values, beliefs, vision, and mission of an organization into the work and lifestyle of team members. Mission attitude and high integrity are applied to the members of the entire team. Spirited leaders rigorously train, model, and mentor the identity consensus of the organization. The "failures" are addressed and corrected using standard practices of compliance, or through basic training and ongoing mentoring.
- In the absence of trust, fear of conflict arises. This is as much the fear of hurting others as of being hurt–the hidden need to "be nice" rather than "focus mission." Leaders challenge the obsession to control and be controlled that often dominates organizational life, and which encourages wasted time seeking permissions from a hierarchy. Spirited leaders monitor compulsive desires to control or be controlled. These are often leftover organizational habits from the past, and they are not overcome simply by "better communication." They are ultimately overcome by clearer executive limitations for team members so that, unless they are expressly told not to do something, they have confidence to take initiative.
- Lack of commitment usually results from inattention or lack of accountability for personal spiritual disciplines. The true team cannot function unless every member of the team merges professional and private life. In a church, this means being highly disciplined about prayer, worship, study, and Godly conversation. In other

---

[1]Patrick Lencioni, *The Five Dysfunctions of a Team* (San Francisco: Jossey-Bass, 2002).

organizations, this means meditation, group morale, continuous education, and interaction with the mission market. Spirited leaders model and mentor the spiritual life and discipline of team members, helping them customize spiritual intentionality for their unique lifestyles. The more the leader attends to spiritual life, the more clear, passionate, and focused the team member will be on mission–and the team member will be less likely to feel overwhelmed by tactical details.

- Avoidance of accountability can be a matter of mission focus, or leadership development, or both. It is revealed either in refusal to be "RAETT-ed" by one's peers in terms of effectiveness and efficiency to live the core convictions and mission of the organization; or in being unwilling or unable to rise to the standard of mission attitude, integrity, skills acquisition, or teamwork demanded by an effective church. Spirited leaders in churches often find this resistance to accountability the most dangerous and also the most difficult issue to address. Churches are generally more merciful than they should be, accepting mediocrity and even ignoring abuse in the idealized hope that people might mature or change. Rigorous grievance procedures can be established to address the potential for abuse, but a deeper sense of courage is needed to confront team members who avoid accountability.

- Inattention to results happens when teams are drawn back into mere program management. They focus on the quality of tasks and the processes of implementation, and measure success by the output of energy or the number of people involved, rather than on the actual achievement of missional ends. Spirited leaders build on the ends policies of the organization to establish measurable goals for the team, and then regularly refer to these expectations in team meetings. They are not uncaring about the problems or stresses on team members, and they can lead the team to solve problems and support one another. Ultimately, however, the team is not the mission. The team leads the mission.

Spirited leaders always ask the team key questions. *Why aren't we being more creative?* The answer lies in the depth of trust. *Why aren't we faster and bolder to develop new mission?* The answer lies in our fear of conflict or anxiety about letting go of control. *Why are team members absent, hesitant, or bored?* The answer lies in the strength of their spiritual disciplines. *Why are teams nervous or angry about standards of behavior and performance?* The answer lies in their clarity about expectations and courage to take risks. *Why aren't we making a bigger impact in mission?* The answer lies in knowing what to measure, and constantly measuring success.

After the Team Meeting

Spirited Leaders know that what happens *after* is just as important as what happens *during* the team meeting. In the simplest teams, members will leave to actually design, implement, and/or evaluate projects following their stage of development. In more complex teams, members will leave to convene other teams for which they are now the leaders. The mission focus and leadership development process from the primary team will be replicated, and insights or training applied to the next level.

The spirited leader can now work as needed with the leaders of any secondary team or project, but without becoming deeply involved in the program management itself.

- *Mentor:* Spirited Leaders will continue to mentor five to seven team members, both as individual and as team leaders in their own sphere of influence. Mentoring guides the team member in spiritual discipline. This is not just about encouragement for prayer or meditation, but guiding the individual to focus mission attitude, grow high integrity, develop essential skills, and learn the art of teamwork.
- *Equip:* Spirited Leaders will continue to train team members, or to guide and support their continuing education path. They can also help team members develop financial resources, or network with other partners within and beyond the church to obtain the technologies or tools necessary to accomplish their missions.
- *Align:* Spirited Leaders will continue to monitor and enforce perfect alignment with the overall core values, beliefs, vision, and mission of the church. They help their team members study the margins, avoid sidetracks, learn from failures, heal the burnouts, and overcome irrelevancy.
- *Intervene:* Spirited Leaders are always available for problem solving, and are always attentive to intervention. There may be an issue to resolve or an unexpected obstacle to overcome. There may be complaint to pass on or a grievance to be explored.

Spirited leaders know that more effective coaching happens when a team member stops the team leader in the corridor with the question, "Got a minute?" than in all of the program management meetings of the old system. The less that Spirited Leaders are absorbed by the details of program management, the more they can be alert to potential threats or sidetracks to the mission.

Conclusion

Spirited leadership keeps the servant-empowering organization fluid. Each team is like a droplet, and each wave is a collection of droplets. Wave upon wave crashes against the cultural landscape, impacts the mission market, and shapes things to come. The last thing spirited leaders want is for the fluidity of the organization to freeze. It will start with just one team, solidifying into a crystalline hierarchy. Of course, it will be beautiful! The heritage property, program, and personnel will please the eye and satisfy the taste, but will no longer shape culture. It will be admired…and ignored…and eventually break apart. Spirited leaders will not allow even a single team to solidify. Every team will be fluid, and the organization will be fluid, and world will be different.

The Power of More

The power of Spirited Leadership lies in what it *wants*, and not what it *is*. This is why traditional organizational job descriptions not only fail to capture the authority of spirited leadership, but actually limit and undermine it. Servant-empowering organizations focus on what the Spirited Leader wants. Servant-empowering organizations refine, clarify, and proclaim that for which the Spirited Leader longs, yearns, and aspires.

The Leader and the Vision

The power of the leader comes from the power of the vision. In a servant-empowering organization, it is never clear whether the leader has clarified the vision, or whether the vision has captured the leader. Traditional organizations perpetuate a false dichotomy between vision and leadership, as if the one can do without the other. Does the leader cast a vision, which everyone follows? Or does the vision emerge from the organizational body, which the leader equips? In reality it is *both* the one and the other. Motivational vision and spirited leader emerge simultaneously. The vision calls forth the leader; the leader discerns the vision.

The Spirited Leader needs a board. In an earlier chapter, I tried to make clear the necessity of the board. The board helps the Spirited Leader discern the future amid ever-changing possibilities and challenges, and formulates the policies that can direct the organization and appropriately deploy leadership and resources to get mission results.

Yet it must also be said that the board needs a Spirited Leader. Indeed, the entire organization requires a Spirited Leader. This is not only because the leader is the "face" of the organization, but also because the leader is the heart of accountability for the organization. Servant-empowering organizations and spirited leadership go together.

Traditional organizations require *professional* leaders. They continually advise the leader not to take the ups and downs, successes and failures of the organization personally. That is exactly why they fail. Their leaders do not hold themselves accountable before God for the success or failure of the organization. Both leaders and organizations believe they can just separate—part company—and both get along just fine. Spirited leaders *always* take organizational vitality *personally!* They know God will hold them accountable for it. Their salvation and organizational success go together.

Readers should not mistakenly assume I am speaking just of the church. This is true for nonprofit and for-profit organizations as well. The "Higher Power" that captures the heart of the Spirited Leader may be differently defined, but the dynamic is the same. Modern corporate leaders treat their organizations as objects to be enjoyed or discarded according to whim and self-interest—and that is why modern corporations are losing market share to non-Western cultures. It is why all organizational life in the Northern Hemisphere is declining. These leaders do not take organizational success *personally.*

The Leader and Power

Leadership is rightly defined by power, but it is crucial to define not two, but three ways power is exercised in the servant-empowering organization. This is best understood in the metaphors of fluidity.

THE POWER OF ONE True Team	THE POWER OF MANY Visionary Board	THE POWER OF MORE Spirited Leader
Stick (Intuition)	Saturate (Shared Experience)	Melt (Transforming)
Drip (Imagination)	Animate (Team Multiplication)	Mold (Shaping)
Merge (Innovation)	Permeate (Community Solidarity)	Meld (Partnering)

Spirited leadership is best understood in the context of the "Power of One" and the "Power of Many," but it is neither the one nor the other. The power of Spirited Leadership is another kind altogether.

THE POWER OF ONE

The Power of One is the power of a team, not an individual. The basic unit of mission is the team, not the office. The singularity that causes the shoreline to erode, and the cultural landscape to change, and the mission market to expand or contract, is the team. The team has real power to discern a mission opportunity and seize it, design a strategy and resource it, implement tactics and do it, and evaluate mission results and start all over again. This is the "droplet" that has power to "stick, drip, and merge."

- Stick to the mission target and begin a chain reaction that will alter its external behavior and internal constitution.
- Drip along the contours of culture, seeping into the crevices of highest opportunity and going around the bumps of highest resistance.

- Merge with other droplets, from any wave, in any direction, so that combinations of energy can accelerate positive change faster.

There is enormous power in the *One,* so long as it is trusted to act. The individual team can be more rapidly responsive, and leverage more change, than any program or curriculum, because they can invent and reinvent themselves for changing circumstances.

The power of a team is limited only by the intuition, imagination, and innovation of the team leader. It is not limited by competencies or resources. If new skills are necessary, the team will learn them. If additional resources are required, the team will find them. The real power comes from the heart and soul of the team leader, and the capacity to mentor and energize team members.

- *Intuition:* The team leader—and therefore the team itself—operates on intuition more than knowledge. He or she anticipates the next challenge, and poises to seize the next opportunity. Intuition does not emerge from a vacuum. Intuition emerges from a disciplined, accountable, spiritual life. It comes from immersion in the spirituality of the organization, and the mission market that is the leader's heartburst. It bubbles within the containment of sacred boundaries of core convictions.

    Intuition is the judicious hunch that one thing will happen rather than another. It is the ability to be one, two, even three steps ahead of the rest of the organization. Like advanced scouts on an expedition, the team discerns the convergence of factors that will precipitate a crisis. Even before the rest of the organization has mobilized, the team has taken the advantage or avoided the confrontation.

    The intuition of the team leader is what makes the team "stick" to its target. Its mission is nuanced to the realities of that particular segment of the mission market. The team leader knows every nook and cranny. He or she can connect the team intimately with the microculture.

- *Imagination:* The team leader—and therefore the team itself—is guided by imagination more than certainty. He or she instantly sees tactical possibilities. The leader deconstructs and reconstructs his or her limited resources, and then goes out and acquires more resources from the most unlikely places. Imagination looks beyond the nooks and crannies of a particular mission market, to see the larger picture of networks and leverage points that reach the next particular mission market.

    Imagination is the inspired realization that *this* set of possibilities will create more mission results than *that* set of possibilities. It is the ability to picture the internal and external relationships of the future under circumstances that can be controlled by the team.

    The imagination of the team leader is what makes the team "drip" along the contours of culture. The team probes, explores, experiments, and travels from one opportunity to the next. The team leader follows a map in his or her mind.

- *Innovation:* The team leader–and therefore the team itself–is committed to innovation rather than preservation. He or she is convinced of the reality of change. New realities demand new tactics. New tactics may build on old tactics, but they are still new tactics. The priority is not to preserve tactics but to get results.

  Innovation is not really a matter of doing something completely new. It is a matter of borrowing from diverse sources, and using old things in new ways. Invention is only a brilliant extension of previous discoveries. Innovation is the process of building invention on top of invention.

  The innovation of the team leader is what motivates the team to "merge" strategies, partnerships, and resources in original ways. The team exercises a radical pragmatism about the past. The more fearless the team leader is, the more creative the team becomes.

The Power of One is the power of a single team to transform any given microculture, and then create a cascade of change from microculture to microculture to impact the entire mission market. The team, not any particular individual, exercises considerable power to discern, design, implement, and evaluate mission.

THE POWER OF MANY

The Power of Many is the force of wave upon wave beating against the shore. It is the power of dozens, hundreds, and millions of teams, synchronized to accomplish one great purpose. Teams are united in a single consensus of core values, bedrock beliefs, motivating vision, and strategic mission. They work in unity, play in unity, sleep in unity, and live in unity. There is not a single moment of any day when they are not in unity. Their purposefulness is persistent, constant, and relentless. This is what erodes the seashore and sculpts the cultural landscape.

- *Saturate:* The Many saturate the mission market with their core convictions and purpose. The organizational presence is felt in every sector of culture: religious, social service, health, business, government, law, education. It is impossible to be unaware of the existence of the organization's vitality, or indifferent to the organization's purpose.

  Saturation means "shared experience." The experience of God (however that Ultimate Concern or Unconditional Loyalty is described) cannot be fully explained by the rationalizations of authorities or the definitions of sociologists. The purposefulness of the organization cannot be fully contained by the regulations of bureaucracies or the stereotyping of public opinion. It is "shared" throughout the mission market; and it has to be "experienced" to be understood.

- *Animate*: The Many animate the mission market, destabilizing life, raising stress, and creating restlessness for change. Culture awakes to new possibilities, hopes, and dreams. This animation is both evolutionary and revolutionary, and the difference is only a matter of speed. Sculpting the cultural landscape may happen through many subtle alterations of sand, or sudden landslides.

  Animation means "team multiplication" through the acquisition and involvement of new team leaders and new team members. The Many gather momentum because people are attracted beyond any individual team to the organizational vision itself. Indeed, they are astonished by the freedom they have to form new teams, going in new directions, under the impetus of a single motivating vision.

- *Permeate*: The Many permeate life. They create a flood zone that erases the boundary between land and sea. Organizational vitality and purpose become united with cultural vitality and purpose. Every aspect of life and work is connected with the mission of the organization.

  Permeation means "community solidarity." The artificial boundary between mentor and seeker, seller and consumer, gives way to a larger community of believers and owners. People exchange roles, and move in and out of various modes of organizational participation, without ever leaving the organization itself.

The Power of Many is the power to go beyond "institution" to "movement," or to return from the solidity of institutional preservation to the original fluidity of missional movement. This power is exercised most concretely by the board. It is the board that has authority to define the cost of discipleship. On behalf of the organization as a whole, the board sets the price the organization should be willing to pay to fulfill its vision in the future. As the Many gather momentum, individuals are increasingly swept away by the power of the vision.

THE POWER OF MORE

A third locus of power lies, however, beyond the Power of One and the Power of Many. If organizational authority is limited to these two powers alone, the organization will lose fluidity and become solid, immovable, and institutional. Teams will become task groups, and boards will become administrators. Impressive mission impact will not be sustained, but gradually weaken. The sea will calm, and the cultural landscape will remain unchanged. A status quo between sacred and secular, or between organizational identity and mission market, will emerge. Why will this happen?

- It will happen because teams will become satisfied. The most intuitive, imaginative, and innovative teams will succeed, and then fail to follow up on success. They will grow complacent. They will rest from their hard work. They will look upon the sea not as a turgid chaos of creativity, but as an oasis beside which they can rest and celebrate their laurels.

- It will happen because boards will become proud. The most visionary, results-driven, sacrificial boards will achieve results, and then fail to risk their profits. They will grow selfish. They will raise their own salaries. They will look upon the sea not as relentless waves of purposeful energy, but as a stable resource from which to draw their pensions.

So long as no third power exists, the Power of One and the Power of Many will eventually lose power to influence and expand the mission market because of the innate self-interest of human beings. If we look to ancient times, this is exactly what happened. The Israelites barely made it to the promised land, and once settled they lost purposefulness. The earliest Christian mission became an established religion, and once certified they lost purposefulness. Mission impact gradually eroded. If we look to contemporary times, this is exactly what is happening with church, nonprofit, and for-profit organizations. Religious institutions are busy protecting heritages, nonprofits are busy defending turf, and for-profits are busy protecting pension funds. All have lost touch with the original creative chaos from which they emerged. All lack purposefulness.

Organizations demand a third locus of power, beyond the One and the Many. Israel needed a Moses or a Golda Meir. The Christian church needed a Paul or a Martin Luther. The nonprofit needs a Martin Luther King Jr. The for-profit needs a Jack Welch. The point is not that every organization should embody the particular values or beliefs of these peculiar leaders, but that organizations demand their sense of relentless purposefulness. The third locus of power is the desire, yearning, passion, and calling of a Spirited Leader. The Spirited Leader holds teams and board accountable to an ever-evolving vision and mission. The Spirited Leader sparks the readiness of teams *never* to be satisfied, and the readiness of a board *never* to be overconfident. Spirited Leaders move organizations beyond complacency.

Spirited Leaders always want *more*. That is the fundamental authority they bring to the organization. They want ever more rigorous alignment with mission. ever more seriousness of integrity. ever more quality in performance. and ever more creativity in teamwork. They want more impact. They want more results. This urgency about mission is what drives them, and the organizations they lead, to take more risks, make more changes, connect with more microcultures, and achieve more success.

- It may make the Spirited Leader appear merciless toward staff and volunteer leaders, but this is not a lack of compassion for people inside the organization. It is an overabundance of compassion for people beyond the organization. It is not a lack of appreciation for organizational members, but a more radical concern for the world beyond the organization.

- It may make the Spirited Leader appear egocentric, but this is not megalomania for self-aggrandizement. Indeed, Spirited Leaders generally cut their own salaries first in hard times, and most perfectly model the sacrifices required for success. The drive "for more" is really surrender to the depth and breadth and power of the larger vision.

Spirited Leaders are simply never satisfied. They are never arrogant. They are simply driven by a vision that is greater than themselves, greater than the organization, and greater than all the multiplying mission markets put together.

The Spirited Leader brings a crucial third power to the organization. He or she provides the drive and urgency to organizational life. The leader makes it possible for the One and the Many to stick and saturate, drip and animate, merge and permeate without stopping or slowing down.

- *Melt*: The Spirited Leader is constantly intervening to break control, overcome stagnation, shatter complacency, and replace satisfaction with restlessness. Conflict resolution is not a role for spirited leadership, because spirited leaders actually fear and avoid harmony. They prefer barely contained chaos—chaos that is only contained by boundaries of core values, beliefs, vision, and mission.

  Whenever the liquid organization is in danger of solidifying or crystallizing around offices and bureaucracies, spirited leaders "melt" the organization. They turn up the heat. Whenever the organization is becalmed, so that waves are no longer generated and droplets no longer erode the cultural landscape, the spirited leader disturbs the water—or, the vision disturbs the water, and the spirited leader discerns it. It's one and the same thing.

- *Mold*: The Spirited leader is constantly shaping and guiding the growth of more leaders. The flow of personal growth and leadership development is the Spiritual Leader's singular passion. He or she is constantly mentoring organizational members to become leaders, and organizational leaders to become better leaders. The Spiritual Leader shapes both professional and private life into a single, mission-driven lifestyle.

  The organization is like wet clay or melting snow. It can be carved and compacted, molded into new forms and original shapes, curved around obstacles, and channeled toward new destinations. Organizational members can be trained, staff can be deployed and redeployed, and the organization itself coached to change heritage, attitude, assets, and programs to move in new directions.

- *Meld:* The Spirited Leader is constantly building relationships for mutual mentoring, support, education, tactical implementation, and critical evaluation. Droplets and waves can be blended together to be more effective, without jealousies and egos getting in the way. The leader removes program silos and creates seamless unity of purpose.

Melding goes beyond facilitating cooperation. It is about integrating personalities and bonding hearts so that organizational members think and act as one. The Spirited Leader guides the organization to surrender even its own success to the driving force of the vision.

Conclusion

The desire for more is the essential authority of spirited leadership. More what? More depth and more mission. The Spirited Leader wants the organization to surrender more deeply to the vision. He or she compels organizational members to go deeper into "God," the sacred experience of ultimate loyalty and ultimate concern that lies beyond the organization itself, and to which the organization is but a servant. The Spirited Leader wants the organization to go further in mission. He or she compels organizational teams and boards to reach the next microculture, expand to the next neighborhood, and touch the most remote mission market. Spirited Leaders are all about the business of going "deeper-further."

The Spirited Leader completes and unifies the servant-empowering organization. The Spirited Leader is personally responsible to model and maintain the synergy of vision, surrender to the vision, and pursuit of the vision. In the end, the servant-empowering organization shapes itself around rigorous alignment, leadership development, and inexorable mission. These organizations will last a long, long time, and they will change the face of the earth.

The Future of the Servant-empowering Organization

The emerging trends of the postmodern world suggest that the basic principles of the servant-empowering organization will permeate every sector of society. Simply stated, we are moving toward a kind of perpetual chaos in which *fluidity* is simply more useful that *solidity*. Fluid organizations will be more adaptive, relevant, and productive in the emerging chaos that solid organizations. These trends toward chaos include:

- *Speedy decision-making:* Information travels swiftly and precipitates instant decisions. Yet these decisions need to be made wisely, by leaders who have the freedom, power, *and* trust to discern, design, implement, and evaluate tactics. Hierarchies based on program maintenance will not be able to keep pace with the lightning speed of shared information. Opportunities and liabilities overtake or overwhelm the slow-moving solid organizations of the past. Only the fluid organizations that focus on leadership development can position and empower leaders to make rapid decisions well.
- *Immediate accountability:* Course corrections occur constantly. Yet these corrections to corporate habits, tactics, and resources must be made judiciously by leaders who can hire, train, evaluate, and fire team members as needed. Bureaucracies with centralized personnel practices will allow unaligned, untrustworthy, incompetent, or egocentric leaders too much time to irreparably harm the organization. They will also allow too much time for passionate, committed, capable, and cooperative leaders to become frustrated and leave the organization in their dust. Only the fluid organizations that decentralize accountability can simultaneously avoid litigation and accelerate productivity.
- *"Glocal" interconnectivity:* Alliances and partnerships not only change quickly, but also span macro-cultures and permeate microcultures. This constantly changing ferment of networks has replaced "divisions" and "departments" in the solid organizational structures of the past. Compatibility, however, can no longer be taken for granted. Only the

153

fluid organizations that are constantly searching, adjusting, merging, and separating can have the radical pragmatism to be effective.

- *Holistic spirituality:* Just as cubicles are giving way to cell phones and text messaging, so also the boxes into which we bracketed off aspects of our existence are being removed. My space has become just one, vast, open space of body, mind, and spirit; work, play, and intimacy; personal fulfillment and professional productivity. Only the fluid organizations can offer the opportunity to unite daily life with infinite meaning and allow the daily grind to become transparent to surprise and aligned with calling.

The emerging chaos cannot be contained by bureaucracies, but neither can they be controlled simply by individual charismatic super-executives. What is needed is a new organizational life that is fluid enough to adapt, yet empowers manageable waves or continuities of movement that endure across generations of executives and teams and preserve essential integrity and purpose.

The metaphor of ocean waves repetitiously pounding the shoreline of the cultural wilderness is the best way to capture the larger picture of this organizational fluidity. The surf is white with creativity, as teams are sprayed against the shoreline; yet the ocean's power lies in the continuous rollers and originates in the hidden depths of the sea.

The Empowering Organization

Prescriptive

Identity
Define, refine, celebrate

Organizational Gathering
Consensus
Leadership Credibility

Accountability

Expectation
Vision Refinement, Policy, and Price

Board of Directors
Focused Consensus
Mentoring

Productivity

Management
Embedded Consensus
Volunteer Empowerment

True Teams
Applied Consensus
Freedom to Innovate

Training
Human Resources, Training, and Administration

Proscriptive

Tactics
Mission Adaptability, Alignment, and Results

The rear of the wave (the "swell") is where leaders are developed in the fluid organization. The stored energy of the wave is gathered, focused, trained, and thrown against the shoreline of the cultural wilderness. Visible in the "swell" of the wave is the light playing on the surface of the water, the color and opacity of the ocean. This is the spiritual consensus of the organization around core values, convictions, vision, and mission that is embedded in the heart of every leader. It is what is modeled by the board and staff to make them credible leaders. Invisible in the "depths" of the wave is the undertow that tugs and pulls leaders to be accountable. This is the invisible, sometimes painful process of aligning mission attitudes, building high integrity, training competency, and forging teamwork. In the "swell" and the "depths" of the wave, leaders are empowered and trusted.

The front of the wave (the "crest") is where leaders are thrown out or sprayed to accomplish their mission and sculpt the cultural landscape according the purpose of the organization. The vision or purpose is clarified, focused by policy, and risked against the potential of failure. This is the position of the visionary (non-management) board, as they survey the future and discern opportunities and liabilities. The droplets of water that spray outward from the wave are the many different teams, each one a self-determining unit, designed to stick, drip, and merge as they impact the mission market. These teams apply the consensus of spirituality to the realities of the cultures the organization is trying to reach. They are highly adaptable, profoundly trustworthy, and abundantly fruitful.

The movement of the fluid organization from left to right is a flow from accountability to productivity, which then draws the various teams back into accountability. Leaders are developed and then launched, returning to the depths of the organization to be renewed, retrained, and redeployed over and over again. What happens visibly at the top of the wave is "prescriptive." That is, the organization defines the identity and purpose that every team reveals and with which every droplet must align. What happens invisibly at the bottom of the wave is "proscriptive." That is, the organization defines the limitations beyond which no team can go. This protects safety, guides learning, and insures cooperation.

Therefore, the fluid organization is not defined by structures, but rather by "dynamics." A "dynamic" is movement or flow in the life of an organization that is constantly repeated, yet subtly different every time. It is predictable in its occurrence, but unpredictable in its result. Fluid organizations have three fundamental dynamics:

- Identity and teams (foundation of trust and trustworthy agents)
- Board and management (visionary leaders and leadership training)
- Spiritual leadership (mentored teams and spirited mentors)

If any of these dynamics breaks down, the wavelike relentlessness of the servant-empowering organization slows down. Soon the water becomes calm and even freezes over. Fluidity crystallizes into solidity. To become fluid again, each of these dynamics must be restored. Identity and purpose must be reenergized, and teams turned loose. Board members must step up to a higher standard of spiritual discipline and stake their lives on a larger mission. Management must learn to refine, embed, align, team, target, and let go. Spiritual leaders must take responsibility to mature members and aspire to greatness.

The following is a composite example of a liquid church. Since the servant-empowering organization can and must be customized for the unique spirituality and mission market of any church, there is no one single blueprint. Yet in this example, we see the elements of organizational fluidity, and we can study the stresses and challenges of the church that attempts to "unfreeze," "thaw out," and transform the "dead calm" of institutional life into a "roiling ferment" of mission movement.

Here is the snapshot of what happens to leadership deployment in the wave. The heart and soul of the servant-empowering organization is high trust. This is the "spirit" of the organization that is embodied most particularly in the senior pastor and visionary board, and which is embedded in all leaders and members. Around this sacred trust is shaped the discipling process in which people are being changed, grown, targeted, and sent.

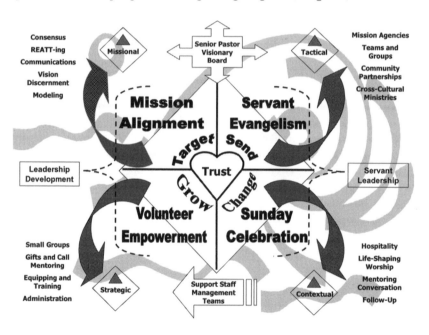

In the fluid circular movement of the wave, one can start anywhere to explain the leadership deployment strategy. The best way to encounter organizational leaders is to begin where the public finds them first. After all, it is the chaotic surf and the spray of the organization that most attracts attention.

The public first encounters organizational leaders through the deployment of teams. (See the upper right of the chart and move clockwise). These teams may be called mission agencies or small groups. They spray in multiple droplets to strike the shore of the cultural wilderness. This particular chart is oriented to churches, but it is equally relevant to speak of "servant evangelism" for nonprofit agencies and for for-profit corporations, because team leaders are trained not only to be productive but also to communicate good will. They share the spirit of the organization–articulating and modeling its core values, beliefs, vision, and mission. They communicate the essential spirituality of organizational life, even as they do things that positively alter the lives and lifestyles of the public

These "servant leaders" do not directly serve *the public,* since the public may not really know what it wants or needs. They do serve the higher vision of the organization that wishes to bless the public, and the positive ends that they hope will result from their mission. These teams interact with the mission market, drawing people toward a primary mentoring experience. For the church, this is most likely going to be the "Sunday morning experience" that includes radical hospitality, life-shaping worship, and all the significant conversations that emerge spontaneously and strategically between mentors and seekers. In other nonprofit and for-profit organizations, there will be some other primary way in which the leaders and mission market interact in mentoring moments.

Like the undertow of the wave, servant-empowering organizations draw the public back into the inner life of the organization. Team leaders "hand off" constituent publics to the support and management staff that mature volunteers through various small groups and training processes. Volunteers are guided to discover gifts and discern personal vocation, equipped with skills and teamwork abilities, and empowered to be future risk-takers and team leaders.

As volunteers emerge at the surface and join the "swell" of the wave, leaders embed the foundation of trust that is the consensus of the organization. Senior staff, pastor, and board model the spirited life and competencies required for mission. The emerging leaders are taught the process of accountability known as "REATT-ing" (refine, embed, align, team, and target), and learn to align personal mission with the overall vision of the organization. They are accelerated by the "swell" of the wave to be released into teams, groups, and mission agencies that are sprayed like droplets from the crest of the wave. Each drop can "stick, drip, and merge" to impact mission market and shape the cultural landscape.

Throughout this process, the public has encountered various layers of leadership. Although the explanation seems very linear, these encounters with leaders are messier than one might think. These encounters are as much about "mentoring moments" as "continuing education processes." Note especially that the senior pastor (or organizational executive officer) and the visionary board locate themselves in the swell and crest of the wave— not in the spray and undercurrent of the wave. Their role is to accelerate and target maturing volunteers to take initiative for mission. They orient themselves toward the depth of the wave to protect the foundation of trust; they orient themselves toward the future, clarifying the vision and anticipating how the vision will intersect with ever-changing cultures down the road.

Now refer again to the chart, and notice the diamond shapes at each corner. These compliment one another. The dynamic of consensus and teams links the "swell" and the "spray" of the organization. This is the movement between mission and context. Missional targeting guides contextual implementation; but contextual experience continually refines missional targeting. The dynamic of board and management links the "crest" and "depth" of the organization. This is the movement between strategy and tactics. Executive limitations for safety, teamwork, and continuing education guide entrepreneurs; but entrepreneurs continually test and shape executive limitations.

Leaders are deployed differently in each quadrant of the fluid organization. Gone are the old distinctions between "senior" and "junior" staff, the old separation between "executives" and "secretaries," and the old dichotomies between "salaried staff" and "volunteers." Instead, leaders are deployed with reference to their role in policy governance. Everything that occurs above the horizontal line, in the "swell" and "crest" of the wave, relates to ends policies and organizational habits; everything below the line, in the "spray" and "depth" of the organization, relates to executive limitations. Everything to the right of the vertical line, in the "crest" and "spray" of the organization, relates to extreme productivity. Everything to the left of the line, in the "swell" and "depth" of the wave, relates to rigorous accountability. Leaders are defined by the quadrant in which they work. They are not defined by the tasks that they do, or the number of people that they lead, or by the seniority of their tenure. The flow, the movement, of the wave is a great equalizer.

The servant-empowering organization is fundamentally a force for leadership development. The programs will come out of the leaders. It is not an engine for program maintenance. Leaders are never recruited simply to implement tasks. The greatest danger for a "solid" organization is that a program may be underfunded; the greatest danger for a "fluid" organization is that a leader may be underdeveloped. If any one of the four quadrants becomes ineffective, the wave motion of the organization will disintegrate. The sea of creativity will become calm. The cultural landscape will remain the same. The mission market will be untouched.

- If the dynamic of consensus and teams disintegrates, mission alignment and contextual adaptation falls apart. Leaders cannot align themselves rigorously to the essential spirit of the organization. The mission no longer shapes the context, but the context dictates the mission. Change happens for the sake of change, or, more accurately, change happens according to the personal biases of teams and the cultural comforts of the context, but there is no overarching purpose.

- If the dynamic of board and management disintegrates, strategic planning and tactical implementation fall apart. Leaders are no longer poised to seize emerging opportunities, but implementation crises drive decisions. The organization becomes reactive, rather than proactive. Since there is little or no equipping, there is little or no mission impact.

- If the dynamic of spirited leadership disintegrates, the pastor/board relationship with team leaders falls apart. Leaders are no longer held accountable to the shared trust at the heart of the organization. The organization falls back into by-laws, redundant oversight, and prescriptive thinking. Staff leaders become interchangeable parts in an ecclesiastical machine (or expendable parts in a corporate hierarchy). The organization (congregation) loses control over its own destiny and is vulnerable to the changing winds of multi-national corporate interests or denominational politics.

If any or all of these things happen, the organization loses momentum. It no longer makes waves in the mission market, and its teams no longer crash against the cultural landscape. If anything, the gradual erosion of culture fills the calm organizational waters with silt and sand.

Intervention can happen in any or all of the quadrants on the chart. It may be difficult for organizational insiders to discern just where the leverage point is that will stir the organizational waters and "make waves" in the mission market. Often it is the foundation of trust that has been lost and now must be recovered. Perhaps this is because the pastor or CEO has retired or been replaced, or the board no longer models the spirit of the organization and surrenders to a greater purpose. Perhaps the problem lies with the "undertow" in the depths of organizational life, so that volunteers are no longer being "handed off" to other mentors and are being held captive in program silos. Perhaps the equipping and training processes have decelerated in an atmosphere of contentment, or the expertise that is being trained is no longer relevant to the changing mission market. Whatever the reason, appropriate intervention can disturb the creative waters once again to make the organization effective in mission.

Organizations are remarkably sensitive to the "climate" of culture. One wonders what might happen if a new "ice age" results from global warming. What if the mobility of people changes for lack of gasoline, and public movement is once again limited to the neighborhood? Will we see a return to the old "solid" organizations like the neighborhood parish and the business bureaucracy? What if the Internet crashes, and "glocal" networking slows down for lack of communication? Will we see a return to the "solidity" of denominational franchises and department stores? I do not think so. The "fluid" organization is here to stay. We have been introduced to the simplicity, accountability, and effectiveness of servant empowerment and most people will not want to go back. It would be like the ancient Israelites turning back to Egypt; or the American pioneers who experienced "life, liberty, and the pursuit of happiness" returning to eighteenth-century England. Some may do so, but it will have more to do with their desire to be cared for rather than their desire to care for others. It will have more to do with defensive anxiety, protecting comfort zones, and avoiding the hard work of personal growth and leadership development. Most will never go back. The lure of spiritual purpose, personal development, and leadership opportunity will always beckon them to a different kind of organization.

APPENDIX

Evaluating Purpose

Introduction

The servant-empowering organization has a clear consensus of core values, bedrock convictions, motivating vision, and strategic mission. This functions as a "foundation of trust" for the innovation of all teams and accountability of all team leaders.

The purpose of this discernment process is to help organizational leaders answer two important questions for the future of their shared ministries:

1. Is our statement of values, beliefs, mission, and vision really effective?

Is it clear? Is it comprehensive? Is it motivational? Does it precisely reveal all that we are and all that we desire to be? Will it help us be faithful and fruitful?

2. Is our organization designed around that statement really efficient?

Does our structure work? Are our leaders and resources deployed in ways appropriate to the statement of vision, mission goals, and core values?

The identity and vision of an organization are only really embedded when every organizational unit (leader, program, project, team, budget line, property, etc.) is truly aligned. Each unit reveals fully the core values and convictions of the organization...and nothing else. Each unit pursues the motivating vision and strategic mission...and nothing else.

The process we will use involves intentional research and conversation at every level of leadership in the organization. This includes meetings for staff, board, management, teams, and other groups. Results will be collated and shared.

- The *Organizational Alignment* tool, "REATT's" organizational structure, funding, training, communication, resourcing, and general performance.
- The *Vision Assessment* tool encourages each group to measure how effectively the vision is refined, embedded, aligned, teamed, and targeted.

Consider linking the various meetings of mission units with an ongoing Internet forum so that leaders can trade insights about the strength or weakness of your organizational purpose among all its mission units and partners.

Organizational Alignment

Group Name: _____

Instructions: In reference to the work of *your* group or team, rate yourselves in each evaluation area by agreeing or disagreeing with the statement provided. Use a scale of 1 (totally disagree) to 10 (totally agree). In the final row at the end of each evaluation area, identify what, in your perception, are your team's greatest weaknesses. *Complete this tool silently, as individuals. Your first intuition is usually the most honest.* Then compare and average your scores. Focus discussion on strongly divergent perspectives, and on average scores that are very low or very high.

EVALUATION AREA: STRUCTURE		
CATEGORY	STATEMENT	PERSONAL RATING
Refine	Our mission unit organization perfectly reflects the priorities of our core convictions, vision, and mission.	
Embed	Our mission unit meeting agenda perfectly reflects the priorities of our core convictions, vision, and mission.	
Align	Our mission unit participation perfectly models the priorities of our core convictions, vision, and mission.	
Team	Our mission unit routinely uses the statement of our core convictions, vision, and mission for program and leadership accountability.	
Target	Our mission unit effectively identifies and networks with compatible partners and projects to accomplish mission goals.	

Weaknesses in this Evaluation Area

EVALUATION AREA: FUNDING		
CATEGORY	STATEMENT	PERSONAL RATING
Refine	Our mission unit budget perfectly reflects the priorities of our core convictions, vision, and mission.	
Embed	Our mission unit spending perfectly reflects the priorities of our core convictions, vision, and mission.	
Align	Our mission unit funding perfectly reflects the priorities of our core convictions, vision, and mission.	
Team	Our mission unit is fully trusted to reallocate funds in response to changing needs, opportunities, and constituencies.	
Target	Our mission unit spends money in the right amount, at the right time, for the right programs.	

Weaknesses in this Evaluation Area

EVALUATION AREA: TRAINING		
CATEGORY	STATEMENT	PERSONAL RATING
Refine	Our mission unit intentionally prioritizes teaching newcomers our core convictions, vision, and mission.	
Embed	Our mission unit repetitively asks team members to shape their personal lifestyles around our core convictions, vision, and mission.	
Align	Our mission unit is trained for the highest quality pursuit of our core convictions, vision, and mission.	
Team	Our mission unit is never diverted from focusing and implementing our piece of our core convictions, vision, and mission.	
Target	Our mission unit seamlessly connects with other groups and teams in our church and judicatory, and other mission partners in the field.	

Weaknesses in this Evaluation Area

EVALUATION AREA: COMMUNICATION		
CATEGORY	STATEMENT	PERSONAL RATING
Refine	Our mission unit shares constantly and comprehensively our core convictions, vision, and mission to our partners and publics.	
Embed	Our mission unit refers to our core convictions, vision, and mission in every message and meeting.	
Align	Our mission unit regularly sends and receives updates on the progress of programs in accomplishing mission goals.	
Team	Our mission unit members are always well informed about our progress toward mission goals.	
Target	Our mission unit always tells people what they need to know, when they need to know it, in plenty of time to take appropriate action.	

Weaknesses in this Evaluation Area

EVALUATION AREA: RESOURCING		
CATEGORY	STATEMENT	PERSONAL RATING
Refine	Our mission unit constantly helps our partners contextualize our core convictions, vision, and mission for their own use.	
Embed	Our mission unit places our core convictions, vision, and mission prominently in all resources, in all media.	
Align	Our mission unit always links our work to other partners in local church and judicatory leadership.	
Team	Our mission unit provides sufficient, excellent tools to carry out all our work.	
Target	Our mission unit always provides the right content, in the right media, for the appropriate group.	

Weaknesses in this Evaluation Area

EVALUATION AREA: GENERAL		
CATEGORY	STATEMENT	PERSONAL RATING
Refine	Our mission unit perfectly connects with the diversity of our region, and the speed of change.	
Embed	Our mission unit is "living proof" of the importance of our core convictions, vision, and mission.	
Align	Our mission unit is completely effective in accomplishing what our organization expects us to do.	
Team	Our mission unit is fully empowered to discern, design, implement, and evaluate mission.	
Target	Our mission unit knows what desired results will best measure success.	

Weaknesses in this Evaluation Area

Vision Assessment

Group Name: _____

Instructions: First review the organizational statement of values, beliefs, vision, and mission. Review the many activities in which your group is involved. Familiarize yourselves with the entire tool. Monitor your time to cover *ALL* evaluation areas. In reference to the work of *your* group or team, discuss your answers to the questions in each evaluation area.

REFINE	REFINE STRATEGY
Core convictions, vision, and mission must be tested against the complexity and constant change of our region.	We refine our statement by studying the "margins." Who is left out? What is left out? How does it feel to be left out?
Our Answers:	

EMBED	EMBED STRATEGY
Core convictions, vision, and mission must be revealed in our actual work and the lifestyles of our team members.	We embed our statement by studying our "failures." What didn't work? Who hindered the process? Where did I (we) fall short?
Our Answers:	

ALIGN	ALIGN STRATEGY
Mission unit mandates must be designed, and leaders deployed, for clear mission goals and nothing else.	We align our mission unit by studying "sidetracks." Where do we waste the most time? When do we feel the most doubt? What financial commitments bear the least fruit?
Our Answers:	

TEAM	TEAM STRATEGY
Mission units must be trusted to be radically creative—using values, beliefs, vision, and mission goals for constant accountability.	We assess the quality of teams by studying "burnout." Where is the largest need for volunteers? How do we feel most incompetent? Why do we feel exhausted?
Our Answers:	

TARGET	TARGET STRATEGY
Mission units must focus on those partners and projects that can become "living proof" of our values, beliefs, vision, and mission.	We target our mission unit by studying "irrelevance." Which partners do we ignore the most? Which partners ignore us the most? Which partners have the least resources or weakest tools?
Our Answers:	

ADDITIONAL COMMENTS: